1970

THREE PHILOSOPHERS

THREE
PHILOSOPHERS

By

G. E. M. Anscombe

*Lecturer in Philosophy and Research Fellow in
Somerville College, Oxford.*

and

P. T. Geach

Professor of Philosophy, University of Leeds

CORNELL UNIVERSITY PRESS
ITHACA   NEW YORK

PRINTED IN GREAT BRITAIN

CONTENTS

ANALYTICAL TABLE OF CONTENTS

ARISTOTLE: THE SEARCH FOR SUBSTANCE

'If an eye existed by itself, sight would be its soul.' We
must not object that sight makes an eye only to be *what we*

B

AQUINAS

FREGE

These complex designations can be analysed into a sign for an *argument* and a sign for a *function*. A function is represented not by a bit of print but by what we may call a

ARISTOTLE
THE SEARCH FOR SUBSTANCE

*Καὶ δὴ καὶ το παλαι τε καὶ νυν καὶ ἀει ζητουμενον
καὶ ἀει ἀπορουμενον, τι το ὀν, τουτο ἐστι, τις ἡ οὐσια.*

Aristotle was born at Stagira in Macedonia in 384 B.C., *coming of a line of doctors; his father was physician to the king of Macedon, and, like Aristotle after him, was widely interested in natural science. In 367, his father being dead, he went as a student to Athens, and was there trained in philosophy by Plato. He stayed working in the Academy for twenty years.*

Plato, though he recognized Aristotle as the best brain among his pupils, eventually left the direction of the Academy to his nephew Speusippus. It is often suggested that pique made Aristotle leave Athens. If we are thus to speculate, we might guess that Aristotle's marked lack of homosexuality (as evident in his writings as homosexuality is in Plato's) prevented him from being in every way a success in the Academy.

However that may be, on Plato's death in 347 Aristotle went to Atarneus in Asia Minor, a region where places were sometimes free of, and sometimes under, Persian rule. At that time Aristotle's friend Hermeias had made himself tyrant of Atarneus. Aristotle married his adoptive daughter Pythias. In 344 the cruel death of Hermeias at the hands of the Persians turned Aristotle and his wife into refugees. They escaped to Mytilene, and from there two years later they went to Macedon, in response to an invitation from King Philip to Aristotle to tutor Alexander, who was then thirteen years old.

When Alexander inherited the throne, Aristotle reverted to Athens, where he established his own school in the Lyceum. It was known as the Peripatetic school. Here he taught and pursued his researches into a vast field of studies for the period coinciding with Alexander's career as king and world conqueror. Alexander helped him both with money and by having specimens sent to him from the places where he took his armies. When Alexander died, Aristotle's position at Athens became dangerous; he was threatened with a prosecution for impiety (carrying the death penalty), thus adding one to the list of considerable philosophers persecuted by that city. He withdrew from the place to Chalcis in Euboea and died there in the course of the following year, being sixty-two years old.

Aristotle is traditionally said to have been witty, lively and handsome, with a rather sarcastic expression of face, and something of a dandy. He ends one of his lectures discussing the term 'mutilated' with the remark that a bald man would not be called mutilated; this has been understood to contain a joking reference to himself.

THE extant philosophical works of Aristotle are fairly voluminous in extent, vast in compass, and written in a highly compressed style. From the traditions that we have, it seems possible that they were not written for general publication. Many passages in them, indeed, seem fit for such publication, for though they may be difficult they are highly polished and do not presuppose an initiation into the language and thought of the philosophical schools in which Aristotle taught or against which he lectured. But much else is rendered excessively obscure to us by its allusive character or by the lack of explanation of many phrases which are abnormal Greek and are evidently technical in character.

Many conspectuses of Aristotle's philosophy have been written; I do not want to add to their number. I shall devote the greater part of my account to his theory of substance, predication and existence, because it seems to be the most fundamental and the most central topic in this philosophy; so much so that, apart from Aristotle's account of syllogisms and his ethical, aesthetic and political writings, most of his philosophical work can hardly be understood at all without it.

Part of his fame as a philosopher rests upon his having started the science of logic. He understood his own claim to greatness on this account. 'Of this enquiry,' he wrote, 'it was not the case that part of the work had been thoroughly done before, while part had not. Nothing existed at all . . . If, then, it seems to you after inspection that, such being the situation as it existed at the start, our investigation is in a satisfactory condition compared with the other enquiries that have been developed by tradition, there must remain for all of you, or for our students, the task of extending us your pardon for the shortcomings of the enquiry, and for the discoveries thereof your warm thanks.'

Nevertheless an account of Aristotle's formal logic would, it seems to me, be of only scholarly interest. It falls into two main parts: the treatments of the categorical and of the modal syllogisms. The knowledge given by the first is now well formalised and enclosed in the far wider field of present day logic; and present day logicians

C

are at work exploring modal logic with much more equipment at their command than Aristotle had.

Aristotle himself, however, misconceived the importance of the categorical syllogism, supposing that the theory of it gave him the key to the nature of 'scientific' knowledge. He expresses this view in what I find his worst book: Book I of the *Posterior Analytics*. He supposed that the premises of truly scientific knowledge of anything must be the same as the causes, in the nature of things, of things' being as they are. This led him to characterise as 'sophistic', and not 'scientific', proof, the geometrical method of taking cases and shewing what holds in each one. E.g. if we prove that isosceles triangles have a certain property and that scalene triangles have that property, we have thereby proved that all triangles have that property. Aristotle calls this sort of inference, though it leads to truth because it proceeds correctly from true premises, 'sophistic'—because the demonstration has not been based on the nature of triangles themselves: he wants a syllogism in Barbara here before he is willing to call the knowledge scientific. The example seems to me enough to shew his theory of 'scientific proof' to be something needing the 'pardon' he asks for.

Bertrand Russell remarks somewhere on the fact that logic made greater advances from the middle of the nineteenth century than in the whole period from Aristotle to Leibniz. He says that this shews our superiority to the schoolmen: so great an advance was made by a few minds, whereas in the Middle Ages all the best intellects of several centuries were devoted to the study of logic, but made no advance. The estimate of the comparative advance is beyond question and the explanation simple: the great modern advance in logic waited upon the development of mathematics in order for logic to have adequate tools. On the other hand, it is not the case that the medieval logicians of Oxford and Paris made no fresh contribution to the subject: rather their work ran into the sand and was forgotten. The real oddity of philosophical history is that in the period from the sixteenth to the nineteenth centuries a mutilated and incorrect version of Aristotle's non-modal syllogistic theory, cumbered with nonsensical accretions not to be found in him, was presented as the whole of logic, a finished science. I call these versions of 'Aristotelian' logic mutilated and incorrect because for example they do not take account of Aristotle's remark that 'Every' does not go with proper names, and treat singular propositions as a type of universal propositions. An example of the nonsensical accretions is the well-known doctrine of ' distribution of terms '.

However, as I have said, these matters seem to me to be of no more than scholarly and historical interest. The sole exception here concerns his doctrine of future contingents and a peculiar sense of ' necessity'. He has been thought (e.g. by Łukasiewicz) to have denied that the Law of Excluded Middle holds for future contingents, but this is based on a misunderstanding of his text. If anything, he begs the question in favour of the Law of Excluded Middle. He argues that it could only be correct to say that it was now neither true nor false that there would be a sea battle tomorrow, if when tomorrow came a sea battle neither happened nor did not happen. But he erects a special concept of ' necessity ' according to which what is happening or has happened is ' necessary '—one cannot determine what is already determined, any more than one can make what is already there—whereas one can determine what will be by deliberation and choice. ' What can happen to this coat ' is a phrase introducing a special sense of ' can ' of which this sense of ' necessity ' —in which everything true about the present and past is not merely true but necessary—is the correlate. ' This coat can get torn ' states something other than that ' This coat will be torn ' is a logical possibility—i.e. is not self-contradictory. For ' This coat did get torn yesterday ' is not self-contradictory, but what it says, namely that the coat got torn on a certain date, cannot now come about if, as is indicated by the past tense, we are already past that date.

With so much by way of preamble, I will proceed to Aristotle's notion of substance.

The doctrine of his *Categories* is very straightforward. *First substance* is introduced, and explained in the first place as what neither is asserted of nor exists in a subject: the examples offered are ' such-and-such a man ', ' such-and-such a horse '. A ' first substance ' then is what is designated by a proper name such as the name of a man or of a horse, or again, if one cared to give it a proper name, of a cabbage. A proper name is never, *qua* proper name, a predicate. Thus what a proper name stands for is not *asserted of* a subject.

Aristotle explains the second point, that first substance does not exist in a subject, by giving as an example of what is ' in ' a subject:

' such-and-such grammarianship '. He means that an individual occurrence of grammatical science, such as a particular man's knowledge of grammar, while not being asserted of a subject, exists in a subject. The example is slightly obscure to us; ' such-and-such a surface ' would perhaps be a better one. If we think of a particular surface, such as the surface of my wedding ring, this is not something that is asserted of a subject, but it exists in a subject—namely, the ring. (He explains that when he speaks of things being in a subject, he is not speaking of parts, such as arms and legs which are parts of a man.)

Thus we can see that when he speaks of ' first substance ' Aristotle is talking about what modern philosophers discuss under the name ' particulars ' or ' individuals '. But his doctrine has features not found in modern treatments. The most notable of these are, first the distinction we have just noticed between individuals that do, and individuals, or particulars, that do not, exist *in* subjects (though Aristotle rarely calls what exists in something else an individual, using that term mostly for substances); and second, that he speaks of ' first substance' and ' second substance '. Second substances, he says, are the kinds to which belong the first substances, such as *man, horse, cabbage*.

It will help us to understand this if we remember, and see the mistake in, Locke's doctrine that there is no ' nominal essence ' of individuals. Locke said that if you take a proper name, 'A', you can only discover whether A is, say, a man or again a cassiowary, by looking to see if A has the properties of man or a cassiowary. This presupposes that, having grasped the assignment of the proper name 'A', you can know when to use it again, without its being already determined whether 'A' is the proper name of, say, a man, or a cassiowary: as if there were such a thing as *being the same* without being the *same such-and-such*. This is clearly false. Aristotle's ' second substance ' is indicated by the predicate, whatever it is, say ' X ', that is so associated with the proper name of an individual that the proper name has the same reference when it is used to refer to the same X: with the restriction that the individual is not such as to exist *in* a subject, like an individual surface.

Aristotle says that the definition of the secondary substance (i.e. of the kind X such that being the same individual means being the same X), will be predicable of the individual, and so too will parts of the definition. E.g. ' animal ' is part of the definition of ' man ', and an individual man such as President Eisenhower is an animal. 'Animal' like ' man ' is a name of second substance: this accords well with the explanation I have given, since if a certain proper name e.g. ' Eisenhower ' has been given to a certain animal, namely to that man, then it is rightly applied again to the same (individual) animal. But, Aristotle says, the definition of what exists in a subject is never predicable of the subject. To give an example which fits what he says, if we form a definition of ' surface ' running perhaps 'A surface is such-and-such an ordering of points', being such-and-such an ordering of points is not predicable of the ring which has a surface.

Another example which he gives of what is found in a subject, but not predicated of it, is ' the white '. That is to say, he regards e.g. *the white of this paper* as a particular, just as it is natural to regard *the surface of this paper* as a particular. This is not his language; as I remarked, his ' individuals '—*atoma*—are usually substances and he uses no other word as I am using ' particular '. But in one place at least (*Categories* 1b6–8) his language implies that there are *atoma*, other than substances, which are not *predicable of* anything. If so, it seems legitimate to apply the word ' particular ' so as to cover both individual substances and these other entities which are found in them. Sometimes, he says, the *name* of what is found in a subject can perfectly well be predicated of the subject; this would be an example, for we call the paper white. But the *definition* of what is found in a subject can never be predicated of the subject—that is to say, in this case the definition of the colour white is not predicated of the white paper. Let the definition include the term ' colour '; the paper is not called a colour. (But in the *Metaphysics* he says that strictly nothing but substance has a definition.)

Substances do not have either degrees or contraries; a man is not more a man at one time, less at another, as something is now hotter, now colder; and there is no antipode to man as black is the antipode of white, or hot of cold. These features, however, are not peculiar to substance; for example ' three foot long ' which is not the name of a substance, has neither a contrary nor degrees. *The* most characteristic thing about substances, Aristotle says, is that they are capable of contrary qualifications. That is to say, a man can change from being good to being bad, or from being pale to being tanned, without ceasing to be that man; whereas this white cannot become black— this white would no longer exist if the paper became black.

The example that I have supplied of something existing in a
subject, namely such-and-such a surface, would seem to be a counter-
example; for a surface is not a substance, and yet the same surface
can be now red, now black. To this, however, it can be replied that
since a surface is in a body and hence not a separate substance (*Met.
K* 1060 b 15) the identity of a surface consists in its being the surface
of *this* body; it therefore could not be determined whether a surface
changed from being red to being black, or rather a new red surface
came into the place where a black surface had been, except by determining whether the same body had been first red and then black.

The counter-example considered by Aristotle himself is that of
opinion: an opinion that Theaetetus is sitting down may be first true
and then false, if, while someone is of the opinion that Theaetetus
is sitting, Theaetetus is first sitting down and then standing up. To
this Aristotle replies that this is quite true, but that the change in
question is really in Theaetetus. We can see from this that Aristotle
would reject that *invariability of the truth-value* of a proposition
which is a prominent feature of much present-day logic.

In modern times the understanding of Aristotle's conception of
substance has been impeded by the use of the term ' quality ' to
mean ' simple non-relational predicate '. ' Man ' would then be a
prima facie candidate for being the name of a quality; consideration
however would shew that it takes many different qualities for something to be a man, so ' man ' is interpreted as signifying a complex
of qualities. Then the *substance* signified by ' man ' according to
Aristotle, will be something *other* than what is signified by any
property-word. Thus we find in Sir David Ross: ' Quality no doubt
cannot exist without substance. . . . But no more can substance exist
without quality. . . . The differentia of any substance is a quality. . . .
The substance is the whole thing, including the qualities, relations,
etc., which form its essence.'

Such views are based on the unconscious assumption—which we
have seen in Locke—that one can identify a *thing* without identifying
it as *a such-and-such*—or that if one cannot do this, this is because *we*
are incapable of conceiving substance except as having some qualities.
The thing, then, that is taken to be postulated becomes a thoroughly
mysterious entity which *in itself* has no characteristics: a ' somewhat
we know not what ' which is postulated as *underlying* the characteristics that it is said to ' have ' and which alone enable us to conceive

it. Because Aristotle distinguishes between substance and quality, those who take a predicate like ' man ' to signify a complex of properties readily suppose him to be distinguishing between the being of a thing and the being of any attributes that it has. They then take the thing itself to have no attributes. It would be almost incredible, if it had not happened, to suppose that anyone could think it an argument to say: the ultimate subject of predication must be something without predicates; or that anyone who supposed this was Aristotle's view could do anything but reject it with contempt.

A very great deal of devoted—and extremely valuable—scholarly work in the form of producing texts, commentaries and translations of Aristotle, has been done by scholars impeded by a Lockean conception of substance and an interpretation of ' quality ' as ' non-relational predicate'. Take, for example, Sir David Ross's unqualified pronouncement that the differentiae of substances are qualities. This is based on Aristotle's account of the various meanings of the single Greek word meaning ' what like ? ' or ' what kind of? ' in his dictionary of expressions in *Metaphysics Δ*. ' What kind of animal is man? ' one might ask, and get such an answer as ' a biped '. But it is not to be supposed that every answer to the question ' What like? ' or ' What kind? ' is a predication in the *category of quality*; any more than every answer to the question ' What is . . . ?' is a predication in the *category of substance*. In the *Categories* (3 b 21–2), Aristotle says that the genus (e.g. ' animal ') or species (e.g. ' man ') tell us *what kind* of thing a thing is *as far as concerns substance*: thus the fact that a certain predicate may be the answer to the question ' what kind ' (' what like? '), which is given a restricted use as a label for pre-dications in the category of quality, does not prove that the predicate in question is a predicate in the category of quality.

We can ask ' What is . . . ? ' in connexion with almost any word; perhaps the only exceptions are such words as particles, conjunctions and propositions—the little ' syncategoremata ', connective words, which it takes a certain degree of sophistication so much as to notice. The question ' What is . . . ? ' is a particularly natural form of enquiry where we have substantives—including verbal nouns: ' what is dreaming? ', ' what is a coefficient of expansion? ', ' what is the alphabet? '. The kind of answer that is being asked for by questions of this form is very various. In the first place, it varies according to the subject matter. Further, at a certain stage of puzzlement, the questioner may himself be more or less vague about the kind of answer he wants—as in my first example ' what is dreaming? ', when in a sense he knows what dreaming is, but wants some kind of account of it; what kind of account may not be determined.

Within this very wide range of application of the question ' What is . . . ?', however, we can pick out a sharp and determinate question, to which the required answer is the name of a kind of thing. Yet that expression, ' name of a kind of thing ' is not in itself unambiguously explanatory; we can explain best by giving examples. ' What is iron? ' ' A metal '. ' What is a bird? ' 'A two legged living thing that flies '.

We may also ask, not ' What is . . . ' where our question is completed by a general term, but ' What is *that*? ' Here again we may expect various kinds of answer. E.g. we might be asking for the name of a colour or a shape; or we might be pointing to some concourse of people and require such an answer as ' a May-day procession '. But here again we can pick out that sense of ' What is it? ' that is answered by the name of a kind of thing or of a kind of stuff: ' That is sulphur ', ' That is an oak-tree ', ' That is a hyena '.

Someone who pointed and asked ' What is that? ' meaning ' What is that colour called? ', and who received the name ' cobalt ' from an informant who believed him to be asking what kind of stuff was in a vessel, would be at cross-purposes with his informant concerning the category to which what he was asking about belonged, in Aristotle's sense of ' category '.

' Substance ' is a classification, but whether of things or of concepts (or words) seems difficult to determine. If we ask what falls into the category of substances the answer is ' e.g. men, horses, cabbages, gold, sugar, soap '. This answer mentions things, not concepts or words, so substance might seem to be a classification of things. On the other hand, if we ask in virtue of what characteristics these things are all substances, as we might ask in virtue of what characteristics apples and pears are both fruits, it becomes clear that the cases are quite different. One does not establish that these things are substances by noting anything about them; the description of their properties is already in the form: description of the properties of substances.

I am not saying that it cannot be an empirical question whether such-and-such is a substance. It can; for example, in the case of the sky, or rainbows. But such cases are necessarily the exception. It is not a well-established hypothesis that gold or a cat is a substance: that e.g. the question ' What is it made of? ' has an application to a cat or a lump of gold.

Such considerations as these can only serve as a preliminary indication of the meaning that Aristotle's labour gave to the term ' substance '. Their value lies in three points. First, they clearly fit that explanation of the word which we have derived from the *Categories*. Second, they are in accordance with the rough indication given by Aristotle himself in the *Topics* (102a 33): ' We should treat as predicates in the category of " What it is " all such things as it is appropriate to mention in reply to the question " What is that which is before you? "; as, for example, in the case of a man, if asked that question, it is appropriate to reply "An animal ".' And thirdly, our considerations should help to shew how disastrous to an understanding of Aristotle it is to take the ' quality ' of being winged, say, as an example of a predication in the category of quality as opposed to substance; and in general to suppose that any word signifying a non-relational characteristic or range of characteristics signifies in the category of quality. When Aristotle discusses the *category* of quality in the *Categories*, as we have seen, he does not include in it all the things that might be replied to that one-word Greek question meaning ' What kind? ' or ' What like? '. E.g. he does not include such a predication as ' having six legs ' or ' having wings ' which might be mentioned in reply to the question ' What's the living creature like that's called an insect? ' or ' that's called a bird? ' Such predications of ' differentiae ' he includes, in his discussion of predication, in the category of substance.

We ask ' How are you? ' when we ask after a person's health; now we might suggest an extension of this question ' How? ' to explain the category of quality. It being clear *what* a thing is, there are further questions *how* it is which in a rough and intuitive way we can distinguish from still further questions such as how big it is or what it is doing.

As I have noticed, in speaking of what is ' found in ' a subject—such as its surface or its white colour—Aristotle says that the definition of this is never predicated of the subject. Now he says of the differentia of a substance that the differentia is not something that is in the subject, and its definition *is* predicated of the subject. Can we accept this point as marking the difference between qualities that do, and qualities that do not belong to the *category* of quality, as opposed to the category of substance: what is in the category of quality is *in* the subject, and though its name is sometimes (as in the case of ' white ') predicated of the subject, its definition never is?

This, it is readily objected, will never serve as a criterion for being in the category of quality; only if one has independently decided that the instance of a quality is a particular other than the substance which has the quality, will one be able to say that the definition of the quality is not predicated of the subject. The question will not be settlable by considering whether the subject can lack that quality; for the quality might be some property (in Aristotle's special sense: *proprium*) which is always found in that sort of substance; the idea of *an* ' accident ' as something found *in* a subject is not that of a characteristic that the subject can have or not have indifferently. It may be argued: Only if e.g. Aristotle says that *the white* of a white thing is by definition *a colour*, can he say that the definition is not predicated of the subject; if he were to say that a white thing is by definition a coloured thing, then he would have to let the definition be predicated of the subject. Why should one not play the same trick with what he calls differentiae, such as ' winged ' or ' six footed '? If one called the individual instance of having wings ' this winged ' or ' this wingedness ', and defined wingedness as a certain formation of the skeleton, then since the bird is not a formation of the skeleton, the differentia would become something found in the subject, and would not merely be what was named in answer to *a* question ' what kind ? ' but would be in the category of quality as opposed to that of substance. Thus the distinction within answers to the question ' What kind? ' or ' What like ? ' is arbitrary, unless some other way can be found of determining when something is to be spoken of as ' existing *in* a subject '. It is clear that the question is supposed to be settled by finding out the real definition of the substantial kind in question; whatever differentia is stated in this will be predicated in the category of substance.

Before going further, we must consider what Aristotle is at in propounding his ten categories. These obviously correspond in some way to a set of things which it would make sense to say of e.g. a human being: (1) He is a human being, or he is an animal (substance); (2) He is six foot tall (quantity); (3) He is a bad man; or, He is a cultivated man (quality); (4) He is twice as tall as (relation); (5) He is in London (place); (6) [He existed?] yesterday (time); (7) He is crouching (posture); (8) with boots on (having); (9) is pushing (action); (10) is being pushed (*passio*, suffering, *i.e.* being acted on).

The eighth of these is the one that particularly suggests that the original list was thought out in connection with the different types of things that might be said of a human being; but Aristotle's intention was to find a complete list of fairly simple kinds of things, with significant logical differences between them, that might be said about a subject. It may be doubted whether any such list could be complete. Where, for example, does weight come in? or shape? Into the category of quality; but it might reasonably be held that they were significantly different enough from, say, colour or virtue or education not to deserve to be put together with these; and that these did not deserve to go together themselves. A quality of a body like ' white ' or ' hot ' differs from a quantity in that, for example, you can ask whether it is white or hot *all over*, whereas such a question hardly makes sense for predications of quantity. But if such grounds justify us in speaking of a difference of category, then it looks a hopeless task to construct a complete list of categories; besides, it would be very difficult to decide what predications were simple enough to merit classification as a category; for example, someone suggested that shape is not just in the category of quality, where Aristotle put it in the *Categories* but is 'qualitas in quantitate ', and so presumably belongs to neither category nor yet to an independent one.

It does not look possible to have a system here. On the other hand, the idea of a category-difference, which is suggested by the contrast between predications in one or the other category, is certainly a useful one. When we remember how Plato, with apparent seriousness, argues that there is something contradictory about our terrestrial, changeable phenomena—because Socrates can be first taller than, and then shorter than, Theaetetus without becoming shorter—we see the point of distinctively describing the category of relation.

The different schemes of ' categories ' that have been proposed by philosophers have not really been of the same kind at all, but have had quite different aims in view. To be systematic, a shorter list would seem better, such as was proposed by the Stoics; but a short list will put together what Aristotle is surely justified in separating, such as quality and quantity. Thus there is no rival to Aristotle's list, and so far as I know people have not tried to improve on it by lengthening it.[1] Indeed, here as elsewhere Aristotle has suffered from being either erected into a source of dogmatic truth, or rejected as a source of dogmatic error.

The doctrine of the *Categories* is indeed a relatively crude sketch, upon which Aristotle never improved, while he nevertheless continued to allude to it, as we shall see, in developing his account of *per se* existences in the *Metaphysics*. A *per se* existent in one sense of the phrase is apparently a particular indicated by a predicate falling under one of the categories, and if it is not a substance, it exists ' in ' a substance. While we may find such an expression appropriate for surfaces and even perhaps for colours and shapes, we cannot extend the vague and largely pictorial conception we get by considering these as examples, to the *having on* of boots or the *posture* of an animal or the *action* of kicking or the *passio* of being kicked. Probably the theory of accidents (as the references of non-substantial predicates came to be called) as entities has always been presented to people's imagination simply in connexion with sensible properties. It thus lends itself to representation as a cluster or veneer theory of properties; as if the substance were the lump of underlying material, and the properties a veneer or a barnacle-like cluster of dependent quasi-substances stuck on to the substance. Without doubt the philosophy of substance and accidents has been so pictured.[2] But the picture can only be formed in connexion with sensible, and especially visual,

---

[1] Leibniz has a list which may be a shot at this, introduced with the thesis that the analysis of its members would give us the ultimate simples, which are the most general ideas of all. (I owe notice of this to Miss Hidé Ishiguro.)

[2] Cf. Milton's 19-year-old exercise (Father Ens is addressing his eldest son, Substance):

' Good luck befriend thee, son, for at thy birth
The fairy ladies danced upon the hearth;
Thy drowsy nurse hath sworn she did them spy
Come tripping to the room where thou didst lie,
And, sweetly singing round about thy bed,
Strew all their blessings on thy sleeping head.
She heard them give thee this, that thou shouldst still
From eyes of mortals walk invisible:
Yet there is something that doth force my fear
For once it was my dismal hap to hear
A sybyl old, bow-bent with crooked age,
That far events full wisely could presage,
And in time's long and dark prospective glass
Foresaw what future days should bring to pass:
Your son, said she (nor can you it prevent),
Shall subject be to many an accident.
O'er all his brethren he shall reign as king,

properties. A distinctive mark of this picture, found in Milton's lines on the subject, is that substance is something hidden.

What speaks for a theory of accidents, however, is precisely the demand we may feel for a *reference* for some of those predicates which are not nouns and are not predicates in the category of substance. Quine in *On what there is* says that ' houses ' ' roses ' and ' sunsets ' denote sundry entities that are houses, roses and sunsets, while the word ' red ' or ' red object ' denotes sundry entities that are red houses, red roses and red sunsets. The first part gives us a model according to which we should know how to construct further examples: ' "X" denotes sundry entities that are X's '; and here the term denotes *only* those entities. In the second part, Quine shews embarrassment when he says ' *the word* " red " or " *red object* " '; and what he says gives us no formal model for the construction of other sentences; moreover the things which he says ' red ' denotes are only a few examples. (Aristotle would complain that in explaining ' red ' Quine had added something, incidentally introducing roses, houses, sunsets: cf. *Met* Z 1029 b 33). Yet though I could not complete Quine's list, when I look round I notice some further items which I know I can add to it: red tins, red boards, red curtains, and so on. Might I not construct a formula on the model of Quine's statement about nouns, and say ' " Red " denotes sundry entities that are reds, such as the red of this tin, the red of that book '—meaning, not the (' universal ') shade, but the colour that is the object of vision in each case—which is surely a particular thing?

We can perhaps get at the idea of the Aristotelian ' being *in* a substance ' (except in the case of time) by considering what a change

---

Yet everyone shall make him underling,
And those that cannot live from him asunder
Ungratefully shall strive to keep him under,
In worth and excellence he shall out-go them,
Yet, being above them, he shall be below them:
From others he shall stand in need of nothing,
Yet on his brothers shall depend for clothing.
To find a foe it shall not be his hap,
And peace shall lull him in her flowery lap;
Yet shall he live in strife, and at his door
Devouring war shall never cease to roar:
Yea it shall be his natural property
To harbour those that are at enmity.
What power, what force, what mighty spell, if not
Your learned hands, can loose this Gordian knot?'

is a change in. When butter goes down in price, that is not to say that anything has happened to butter; but when it goes down a chute or melts, something about *it* changes. Thus we might say that apart from the categories *time* and *relation* the list of categories other than that of substance is a list of types of predicate such that a change describable as that predicate's ceasing to hold is a change in the subject. I except time, as the dimension in which change takes place, and relation, because according to Aristotle a change here is always produced by some other change (*Met.* N 1088 a 30—b 1): this is at first sight very plausible, except perhaps for spatial relations.[1] That is why a change in relation may not be a change in one of the terms, but may be produced simply by a change in the other—or again in something else, as when A becomes B's heir by the death of C. The idea of a change which is a real change *in* the subject of a predicate is a vague one, but it seems to correspond to the idea of an ' accident' as something ' in ' a substance, as satisfactorily as perhaps can be hoped for.

Yet it is not difficult to think of predicates a change in which is a change in their subjects, but which certainly fall under none of the categories. E.g. ' defective ' and ' awake '. ' Defective ' because it is, as we should say, second order: it relates to properties some privations of which marks the subject as defective; privation might be said to be reductively in the category to which what it is a privation of belongs, but the term ' defective ' itself would belong to none. 'Awake ' might well be classed as a ' quality ' by a reader of the *Categories*—which shews, if it needed further shewing, how that category tends to serve for miscellaneous predicates not other- wise catered for. But when we learn from the *De Anima* that the soul is the substantial ' form ' of the body, or of the animal whose life it is, and that the waking state is to the soul as actual seeing is to the capacity of sight, it surely begins to look very inappropriate to put ' awake ' in the category of quality. It is a quite different kind of predicate, relating to substantial form and to the potency-act dis- tinction. The non-substantial categories seem to be a rough list, not so much of all the different kinds of predicate, but of different

---

[1] On which Aristotle is, I think, irredeemably archaic. cf. his statement in the *Ethics*, that as ' opportune ' signifies what is good in the category of time, so ' lodging ' signifies what is good in the category of place. This is obviously con- nected with his idea that things have proper or natural places, where they tend to go.

kinds of predicate of a certain very vaguely indicated type—roughly, predicates a change in which is a change in the subject, and the explanation of which does not involve any generalisation over other attributes, as do ' defective ' and ' awake '. Yet the theory of categories is never discarded by Aristotle. A new and far more sophisticated version, written after the *Physics*, *Metaphysics* and *De Anima*, would have been a desirable project, though perhaps an impossible one.

Turning now to the doctrine of the *Metaphysics* we find ourselves confronted with far greater difficulties than are presented by the *Categories*. In a way, I think it is fair to say that Aristotle is groping —even if, as seems to be the case, he thinks he wins through to the truth in the end. This is indicated by the sentence in Book Z which I have taken as the motto of this essay: ' Indeed, the question that was asked long ago, is asked now, keeps on being asked and always baffles us—"What is being?"—*is* the question "What is substance?" '

The first difficulty that we encounter in interpreting this question is this: We naturally—and not wrongly—translate the Greek word *ousia* by the word ' substance ' when we encounter it in Aristotle. But for us this word is soaked with Aristotelian implications; and that not merely when it is used as a philosophical technicality, but in ordinary language too. It is because of philosophy—Aristotelian philosophy—that we speak of e.g. chemical *substances*.

It is, indeed, not in accordance with present *everyday* language to call an individual man a substance; here we are consciously adopting Aristotle's usage. But that is the point: it is for us a *usage*, in which the word suggests a good deal of Aristotelian doctrine. We are ill-placed to understand what it was for Aristotle to arrive at this usage for *ousia*.

As we see, he gives ' What is substance? ' as a gloss on the question ' What is being? ' Confronted with this question we are nowadays likely to ask: 'Are you asking e.g. what existence is, or what the predicative copula means, or what identity is? ' Aristotle's gloss ' What is substance?' does not immediately help us, for the reasons that I have given. What sort of thing did this question mean to him?

We get a glimmering if we remember the Platonic background, which explains the kind of things concerning which Aristotle asks whether they are substances. Are points, lines and planes substances?

Are numbers substances? Do general terms such as ' man ' stand
for substances which are something separate from individual men—
i.e. are there such things as Platonic forms?

It may perhaps help us if we think of the question what *ousia* is
as asking what *entity* is: certainly the questions 'Are numbers, or
lines, or points entities? ' sound much less strange to our ears than the
question whether these are substances—the latter term has acquired
too much Aristotelian significance for us.

Plato uses ' *ousia* ' to mean 'existence', but Aristotle does so very
seldom. For 'existence' he uses the infinitive of the verb 'to be';
this of course also occurs as the predicative copula. When he says
that the ever puzzling question ' What is being? ' is the question
' What is substance? ' the word that I render ' being ' is the present
participle of the verb ' to be ', preceded by the definite article. We
might, then, prefer to render it ' the existent '. Certainly the
participle needs to be rendered as ' the existent ' in this statement
in the second book of the *Posterior Analytics* (92 b 14): ' The existent
is not a class, so existence is not (part of) the substance (*ousia*) of
anything.' The latter sentence would mostly be rendered ' existence
is not (part of) the *essence* of anything.' Thus occasionally the word
' *ousia* ', which is usually rendered by ' substance ' is rendered
' essence ' in translation. Etymologically, the word ' essence ',
which is as it were derived from a mythical participle 'essens' of the
Latin word ' esse ', ' to be ', is close to the formation of ' ousia ' from
the Greek verb ' to be '. The word ' entity ' is a similar formation
from the (classically rare) participle ' ens '. (The word ' substance '
is etymologically more of a rendering of the Greek word for *subject*,
than of *ousia*; however, it came to be the usual translation of Aristotle's
' ousia ', and so to carry with it the Aristotelian suggestions about
ousia.) The difference between ' essence ' and ' entity ' for us is
that the former sounds rather abstract and the latter rather concrete:
though I suppose it would be just possible to render the above
sentence ' existence is not part of the *entity* of anything '. Note that
in speaking of ' abstract ' and ' concrete ' we are using words which
are in our language by inheritance from Aristotelian philosophy.
We shall see that the kind of contrast we feel to hold between ' entity '
and ' essence ' connects up with certain difficulties in making out
what Aristotle says—and indeed with the essence of his doctrine.

In spite of these difficulties about terminology, the thought of the sentence from the *Posterior Analytics* is quite clear. It is: ' There is no such kind of thing as *the things that there are*; that *there is such a thing as it* is not *what* anything is.' So, Schopenhauer remarks, as if with prophetic insight Aristotle forestalled the Ontological Argument of Descartes.

In view of all this, what are we to make of Aristotle's question ' what is being? ' and of his statement that the subject matter of his Metaphysics is ' being *qua* being '? Are we to say, for example, that Aristotle sometimes uses the participle ' being ' to mean ' the existent' and sometimes uses it in some other sense? Or that he changed his mind after writing the *Posterior Analytics*? Such a view might seem to be supported by the doctrine of *Metaphysics Λ* (1072 b 10) that the first cause is ' a being by necessity '. But this would be a misunderstanding. The passage concerns the local motion of the first mobilia (the heavenly bodies). This motion shows that there is some respect, namely place, in which they, whose substance Aristotle thought incorruptible, are capable of being otherwise; whereas there is *no* respect in which the first cause is capable of being otherwise—everything that it is, it necessarily is.

In his dictionary in *Metaphysics Δ* he says that the word ' being ' is used sometimes *per accidens*, sometimes *per se*. The corresponding Greek expressions are of very frequent occurrence in his work. His Latin translators, whose idea of translation was, roughly speaking, transverbalisation, fixed on these Latin renderings. If the same methods of translation were possible in English, we might use expressions, say ' according to supervention ' and ' according to itself ', which, conveying little in themselves, would take on Aristotle's meaning in virtue of the various contexts of their usage. I think it preferable to use one pair of terms everywhere to correspond to the Greek, and so will use the Latin rendering. As we shall see, the phrases have a considerable variety of application.

' Being ', he says, is used *per accidens* when e.g. we speak of a noble's *being* educated or a scholar's *being* noble, or a scholar's *being* a builder, or a man's *being* educated. A is said *to be* B because B (as it happens or, as we might say, as a matter of fact) attaches to A; whether because two things—e.g. *noble* and *educated*—attach to the same man, or because something—e.g. *educated*—attaches to a man. Aristotle stresses a difference between the two cases; the latter is not a case of *man* and *educated* attaching to the same thing. For, as we

D

have seen, he would hold that if one said this, one would have to answer the question ' to the same *what*? '. Now ' man ' is the type of predicate that serves to answer this question; and it would be absurd to say *man* and *educated* attach to the same man. *What* a thing is, is not something attaching to it, or to which it stands in any kind of relation.

His explanation of the use of ' being ' *per se* is that anything is said to be *per se* if the expression for it signifies in any of the various categories (as explained in the *Categories*); for it is the same thing e.g. to say that a man *is* a flourishing one (is physically healthy), and that he flourishes. (Yet he surely cannot be remembering all the ' categories ' in saying this: it would not work for things in the category of time like *yesterday*.)

This may well puzzle us, for could he not as well have supplied this very example as the one he did supply in the explanation of ' being ' when it is used *per accidens*? ' Flourishing,' he could have said, merely attaches to the man, so ' being ' is being used *per accidens* when we say that the man is flourishing.

Let us remember our question: ' When Aristotle asks " What is being? " is he asking what the predicative copula is or what existence is or what identity is? ' We saw that he was not asking what existence is; but he might still be asking what the existent is. All that we know about his view of the question in that sense—assuming him still to have held the view he held in the second book of the *Posterior Analytics*—is that it would not be a question about what kind of things are the things that exist, as opposed to the things that do not exist; i.e. not a question about what distinguishing mark constitutes the existent as existent. Let us put it this way: if there were unicorns, then unicorns would be *ousiai*, entities and substantial entities; but there being or not being such things is *not* what differentiates objects of discourse as *ousiai* or not, or as *per se* existents or not.

I think we are forced to see that the questions ' what is the copula?' and ' what is the existent? ' are not split up for him as they are for us. At first sight we might indeed suppose that when he speaks of ' being ' in a *per accidens* or a *per se* use, he is talking about the copula and trying to distinguish between a use of the copula to make non-essential and to make essential predications: the scholar is a noble because *it so happens* that *scholar* and *noble* attach to the same man, but there is no essential connexion. But if we have assumed that this is what is in question, then Aristotle's account of the *per se* use, which I described above, in the last paragraph but two, throws us into utter confusion.

Now let us suppose that the statement, that a certain man is flourishing, or is educated, is true. If this is so, then a flourishing man, or again an educated man, is among the things that exist, and Aristotle takes it that the copula here expresses this existence. (We should notice indeed that the Greek expression he uses may mean indifferently ' a man is educated ' or ' an educated man exists '.) But, he says, a flourishing man, or an educated man, is not a *per se* existent, but a *per accidens* one; or again, he would say he is not a *per se* unit, but a *per accidens* one. The predicate in ' the man is flourishing ', however, indicates a *per se* existent, and so—he says, surely forgetting about ' yesterday ' as an example of something in a category—is any predicate that signifies in any one of the categories; whether the particulars indicated by them are such as to exist in a subject, or, as holds when the predication is in the category of substance, are identical with the subject. Thus the fact that something exists, i.e. that there is such a thing, does not shew that it is ' an existent ' or ' a being ' in the sense in which Aristotle says that *the* question is ' what is being ?' Terms expressing privation, and terms standing for *per accidens* beings both stand for things that exist, or ' are to be found in the world ', but neither stand for what Aristotle calls ' a being '.

Aristotle goes on to mention as a further use of ' being ' or ' is ' that it means truth; if the dodo *is* extinct, this *is* so. And finally, he speaks of the use of ' is ' (or for that matter the present indicative of another verb) to refer to what is possible rather than what is actual at the time, as when we say (perhaps of a man getting well after an eye operation) that someone is seeing well, because he can see, regardless of whether he is at the moment actually seeing anything; and when we say that certain bulbs are tulips or crocuses, because that is what they can grow into.

To return to the *per accidens* use of ' being '; it is clear that the question ' Is he asking about the predicative copula or about the term " existent "?' must be answered by saying that he does not distinguish here; except in so far as the predicative copula may be used simply to express truth, without carrying with it the suggestion that we are dealing with ' entities ' indicated by the grammatical subject or predicate.

I think it is now fairly clear what Aristotle is saying; but the question remains why he should find it important to say. Also, since in this passage ' being ', and even ' *per se* being ' is not restricted to substance, we are left wondering why he should gloss his questions ' what is being ?' as ' What is *ousia*? '—since there are other things that are ' beings ' besides substances—namely, the things that exist ' in ' substances.

Aristotle's more difficult and abstract writings are plastered with occurrences of certain obscure phrases, which are often rendered in English versions by ' the essence of ', with results that are never illuminating and often quite nonsensical. The phrases in question are of two kinds. The first kind consists of the definite article, the infinitive of the verb ' to be ', and some other word, which is usually a general term, substantive or adjective, but may even be a personal pronoun such as ' you '; and this last word is put into the dative case. Thus we have ' the to be white ', ' the to be man ', ' the to be you ', ' the to be a white surface ', with ' white ', ' man ', ' you ', ' white surface ' in the dative case.

The second phrase goes: ' the what-is-it to be ' (or ' the what it is to be '); this often occurs by itself but may also have a dative attached to it like that of the first phrase.

These constructions are quite extraordinary Greek; they were evidently in familiar use in Aristotle's school as technical terms, and their genesis is a matter of speculation. One cannot hope to understand Aristotle without making up one's mind about what they are supposed to mean, how they work, and quite generally about what their point is.

My own view is that the first type of phrase is in fact historically first and that it has its origin in disputes with the professors of a dogmatic, ' scholastic' type of Platonism. I conjecture that these people were accustomed to say some such things as the following: ' It is really a misuse of language to say that Socrates *is* (a) man (we have to remember that in Greek there would be nothing between the word for ' is ' and the word for ' man ' in the sentence saying that Socrates is a man) or that a given elephant *is* large. For in the first place, the use of " is " suggests that these things—Socrates and the elephant—really *are*, but Plato has taught us that only eternal and changeless things really *are*. In the second place, the only thing that really *is* man is that single kind that the word " man " stands for;

and the only thing that really *is* large is that single kind that the word " large " stands for. These kinds exist apart from the things called " men " and " large ". These things are called so—improperly— to express that they stand in a relation, other than that of identity, to what the words " man " and " large " stand for.'

I conjecture that in reply to this, Aristotle came to devise the formula ' the to be white (dative) ' in the following way. He said something like this: ' In the context of these discussions I will *give* you such phrases as " being white " (where " white " is in the normal case for predication) as meaning (if there is such a thing) *being identical with that separate kind or form that " white " stands for*—so long as you will allow me to say, in the same contexts, not indeed " Snow *is* white ", but " It belongs to snow to be white ".'

In English that does not sound as if it ought to have been particu- larly acceptable to people talking as I have conjectured. But in Greek the word ' white ' in ' It belongs to snow to be white ' naturally goes into the dative by what is called ' attraction ' to the dative case which ' snow ' has after ' It belongs '. Thus the expression might have sounded acceptable and a distinction have appeared to be made between ' It belongs to snow to be white (dative)', which could be admitted, and ' It belongs to snow to be white (accusative)', which less normal construction would be understood as the false statement that it holds of snow that it *is* the White. The sentences (using the dative construction) ' It naturally belongs to snow to be white ' and ' It naturally belongs to fire to be hot ', occur for example in the *Categories* (12 b 39). Nor is the word for ' belongs ' the only one carrying an attraction of a predicate to the dative. I do not wish to suggest that Aristotle's move relied on ' belongs ' alone.

The discussion as I have imagined it does indeed sound primitive or childish. But, in the first place, it is no more primitive or childish than much which we know went on in Greek philosophy, some of which strikes us as such because the special primitiveness is alien to us; and, in the second place, it is true, as someone has said, that in philosophy there is a very frequent temptation to think in a way that a better understanding will want to characterise as primitive or savage. In our own time Bertrand Russell has argued that ' Socrates is a man ' differs from ' Socrates is human ' in that the former is a statement of an identity between Socrates and an indeterminate man; and Prichard racked his brains over how it can be said that an action was obligatory when the action is not, and perhaps will not be, there to possess that characteristic. Still more recently I have heard a similar difficulty raised how some predicate can be going to hold of a subject at a time when the subject perhaps will not exist: as if a man could not be going to be famous when he was dead. Is there not something primitive about the conceptions displayed in each of these cases? It is only when something is primitive in a style in which we are not, that it strikes us as inexplicable how any civilised man should ever have thought in that fashion. Aristotle himself argues that time must be eternal because if we say ' once there was no time ' we are saying there was once a *time* at which there was no time. Opinion must now be divided as to whether this was like the thought of a savage (or say Peter Pan when he wanted his shadow sewn on).

By my conjecture, then, we have Aristotle, for the sake of argument, and with a view to destroying their position, *giving* the ' Platonists ' the expressions ' is A', ' to be A ', etc., to be used to signify being the *form* A, and using another expression, ' being A (dative) ', to signify an ordinary thing's being A in the ordinary way; an accident of Greek idiom made the expressions different. There is some ground for this conjecture in Metaphysics Z (1031 b 5—14). The expression ' being A (dative) ' I suppose to have quickly become divorced from the construction which occasioned it; so it came to be used as an independent noun-phrase of technical import, without the need for any grammatical construction that would justify it.

One of the uses to which Aristotle put his new technical phrase was to attack the doctrine of the Platonists whereby if Socrates is a man, then Socrates stands in some relation to what he is said to be; Aristotle wishes to say: No, he *is* what is spoken of in the predicate. What is that? It is what is signified by his expression ' being man '; as for the other sort of being man, which we may write as ' being Man ', admittedly he is not what, if anything, *that* signifies.

Now one way of interpreting the statement ' he *is* what is spoken of in the predicate ' would be to take ' what is spoken of in the predicate ' as a circumlocutory phrase for the predicate itself; then this phrase itself is used predicatively and the ' is ' is just the predicative copula. Instead of ' Socrates is ϕ ' we would say ' What is designated by the name " Socrates " *is* what is spoken of when we use the predicate " ϕ " ' and this, since the ' is ' is the copula, adds nothing to what we say by ' Socrates is ϕ '. This, however, is not

Aristotle's thought, for it would hold whatever the predicate was. And according to Aristotle, Socrates is not everything that is signified by (true) predicates of him. Let the predicate he ' educated '. Then Socrates and the educated Socrates that exists if ' Socrates is educated ' is true, are one and the same; but that is not the same as to say that being Socrates and being educated are the same, or that being a man and being an educated man are the same.

We have to be very careful not to misunderstand here; Aristotle is not making the merely obvious point that it does not follow from the fact that, if a given man is educated, then he is one and the same with a given educated man, that ' educated ' and ' man ' *mean* the same. For he clearly *does* wish to say that being an animal and being a man are the same, and also that being Socrates and being a man are the same; though it is not at all the case that ' Socrates ', ' man ', and ' animal ' have the same meanings, or that every animal is a man.

His point is that though Socrates and the educated Socrates are one and the same man, if Socrates is educated, still the expression ' educated Socrates ', which stands for something existent, will stand for what is only *per accidens*, since it stands for Socrates-with-education-attached-to-him. Now Socrates and the human Socrates, or the animal Socrates, are not merely one and the same individual, if ' Socrates is a human being ', or ' is an animal ' is true; but what ' the human Socrates ', ' the animal Socrates ' stand for is *per se*, because (a) they do *not* stand for something through the fact that being a human or being an animal *attaches* to the independently identifiable individual Socrates, and (b) ' the human Socrates ' or ' the animal Socrates ' signifies wholly in one of the categories.

It is arguable that no predication except one in the category of substance will indicate being *per se* in this sense. For though the predicates in all the other categories signify being *per se*, yet as soon as they are truly predicated, i.e. attached to a subject, we have what Aristotle calls a being *per accidens*. (An exception that may suggest itself is that of the ' mathematicals '—geometrical figures, lines, points and surfaces, and also numbers; hence Aristotle discusses seriously whether such things are not substances.)

Aristotle reached his position partly from reflection on Plato's theory of forms; we must therefore devote some consideration to the problem set by Plato if we are to understand Aristotle.

Many people who would reject Plato's talk of ' participation ' are yet content to speak of attributes as being ' in common ' among many things which have them. The metaphor is very close to Plato's. If they add that an attribute has no existence apart from the existence of the things that have the attribute—which is the most common opinion—they are still committed to what Plato in the *Philebus* called ' the greatest impossibility of all ', namely that one thing (indicated to us by some predicate ' ϕ ') exists in its entirety, separated from itself, as one and the same at the same time in each of many single things that are ϕ. It exists in its entirety in anything that is ϕ, for it is not shared like a cake, with one bit going to one owner and another bit to another. It exists separated from itself because its existence in this thing that is ϕ is not the same as its existence in that thing that is ϕ. At the same time it is ' one and the same in the one and the many ' i.e. in each of the many single things that are ϕ; for just that is the implication of saying e.g. ' We see *one* thing *in common among* these many things that are ϕ.'

I do not say that as, quoting Plato, I have formulated these problems, they are reasonable problems which genuinely await solution. But these formulations are correct if the talk of ' in common ' has the slightest explanatory force. If it is right to say ' If A, B and C are all red, then this is because they have the property of being red in common, and we learn the meaning of ' red ' by seeing what is common among the red things '—then it is right to formulate those problems just as Plato formulated them. They do not arise in that form merely from his postulating an eternal and separate entity which he called ' the ϕ itself '; they arise in that form as soon as one introduces the expression ' they have something—ϕness—in common ' or ' have the common property of being ϕ ' in the belief that one has said something more than when one says ' These things are ϕ '.

We may perhaps feel inclined to say that 'A, B and C are all ϕ ' is merely repeated in a more laboured style by saying 'A, B and C have the common property of being ϕ' : i.e. to reject as illusory the idea that ' one thing in common among all the ϕs', and similar phrases, have the slightest explanatory force of the kind that has been imagined.

We ought however to qualify this rejection in certain peculiar cases, but the qualification will not affect our point. It will be necessary to digress awhile to shew this. The attribute ' good ' for example has the peculiarity that a good X is good in virtue of being ϕ. and a good Y good in virtue of being ψ. Here there may be some point in saying ' There is *not* a common property indicated by the term " good " '—precisely because many actual attributions of the word ' good ' indicate certain properties (other than ' goodness ') but there are no properties common to all the cases, because different properties are (quite determinately) indicated by these different applications of the word ' good '. E.g. ' a good burglar ', ' a good clock '.

And so, conversely, we might have a use for saying ' the predicate ϕ does indicate a common property in the things that are ϕ ', when the question ' what common property? ' is answered by giving some predicate or predicates other than ' ϕ ', which hold of all ϕ's in that they are ϕs.

It may seem that predicates indicate common properties in this sense only when they are definable, and that we must quickly come to indefinable predicates, which therefore, in the sense we have now given the phrase, indicate no common properties. Such indefinable predicates, however, would not be like ' good ', in the type of application I have mentioned; for ' good ' does indicate certain other properties in each of these various different applications of it as an attribute, whereas the suppositious indefinable predicates would not ever do this; they, it would be held, only indicate the indefinable properties themselves, which they stand for.

In fact, however, the implicit argument for indefinable properties in the last paragraph is wrong; nor do we find any such notion in Aristotle, even though he holds that strictly only substances have definitions. All that can be said is that definitions (and other explanations of a more informal character too) must come to an end somewhere, not that there are particular places at which they must come to an end. So there is in any case no need to suppose that there are indefinable properties. Definition may indeed not always be what we need; but if a property ϕ is such as to indicate common properties, expressed by the predicates ' ψ ' and ' χ ', in all the things that are ϕ, there is no reason to say that with some such predicates ' ψ ' and ' χ ', we must have reached predicates that do not ' indicate common properties ' in all the things that are ψ or χ.

For these reasons it is not off-hand clear that there are any predicates ' ϕ ' of which one must say: there is no common property indicated by the predicate ' ϕ ', in the sense we have now given to the phrase: except for predicates which like ' good ', or again ' game ', indicate now one, now another set of (further) common properties.

In that sense, we will never say that the property of being ϕ is itself the common property indicated by ' ϕ '. And in any case the point of saying that could only be, say, to tell us the grammar of the word ' ϕ '—that it is not, for example, a proper name or a logical constant, but is rather an adjective or common noun.

It may be said that if the common properties indicated by a predicate ' ϕ ', supposing it to indicate any, are properties ψ and χ, then our very form of expression shews that ψ and χ are common properties of things—namely of all the things that are ψ and χ respectively. So the terms ' ψ ' and ' χ ' must indicate common properties. But our expression must be considered as a whole; we should not take a bit of it and draw conclusions from a fancied application of that bit. ψ and χ are properties common *to all ϕ's*, if ' ϕ ' is a predicate indicating common properties in all the things that are ϕ: to say that is to tell us something about ϕ's. It tells us nothing about ψ's and χ's, to say, in addition to saying that they are ψ's and χ's, that they have the common properties of being ψ and χ respectively.

Thus there is a certain use for speaking of the common properties indicated by a certain predicate, as also for denying that some given predicate does indicate properties common to all the things to which it can be applied. This, however, does not affect our main point, to which we can now return. We can grant this sense in speaking of common properties, and still hold that there is no ground for the statement that leads to Plato's problem. We can say that we see no ground for passing from 'A, B and C are all ϕ' to 'A, B and C have the property of being ϕ' and from that to ' The property of being ϕ is something in the Universe: it is the kind of thing called a universal, or concept, or by some a general idea '. (Cf. G. E. Moore, *Some Main Problems of Philosophy*, pp. 301–5).

Now if we take this line, we have not shewn that there is no question of real existences indicated by general terms used predicatively. Aristotle at any rate does not take this view. His solution is the following: certain predicates (i.e. the ones that fall under one or another of his ' categories '), when truly applied to a ' first substance ', indicate an existence or an existent; I do not know which expression is the apter. When the predicate is in the category of substance (e.g. ' man '), the existence indicated is the very same as the existence indicated by the proper name (e.g. ' Socrates ') of that first substance which is the subject of the predication. When the predicate is in some other category (e.g. ' white '), we get a distinction which does not exist for the category of substance: a *per accidens* being (e.g. a white man) is indicated, which would be indicated also by the combination of the predicate as an adjective with the proper name (e.g. ' White Socrates '); but also a *per se* existence, which is other than the existence indicated by the proper name. But in no case is any *per se* existence or existent indicated other than that indicated by the proper name of a ' first substance ' or than that (which has no proper name) which occurs ' in ' a ' first substance '—e.g. the surface of this paper which exists in this paper: or again, the white of this paper.

Aristotle's argument against Plato (inspired by Plato's own arguments in the *Parmenides*) is this: Plato held that all (or almost all) general terms stood for ' substances, natures, ideas ', which were other than and existed apart from the particular things that partici-pated in them—or, as we should say, had them in common. The many good things have the good in common, the many beds the bed, the many yards the yard, the many animals the animal, and so on—we must even say that the many beings have the being in common. Now the yard will certainly be a yard long, the good will be good, the being will be, the animal will be animal. Then the existences indicated by the predicates in *these* sentences ought to be identical with the subjects; for otherwise we are in for another set of ' sub-stances, natures, ideas ' behind the first lot. Thus in any case there have to be entities and predicates such that the entities are identical with the existents indicated by the predicates—which is enough to shew that it was superfluous in the first place to postulate ' substances, natures, ideas ' prior to and distinct from the ' first substances ' in Aristotle's sense, with which we started.

Aristotle is sometimes said to have believed in the ' universal ' as existing *in rebus*, as opposed to Plato's belief in the ' universal ' as existing *ante res*. That is, Aristotle is supposed to have held the view which Plato described as ' the most impossible of all '. I think this is a calumny on him. It would be closer to his view if we ascribed to him an alternative that Plato proposes: namely, that a single form is divided up and becomes many, or, at least, that the situation is *as if* a single form had been divided up and become many. Thus if there were only one large lump of gold in the world, the division of it would make gold, which had been only one thing, become many. The division, it may be protested, is material—a division of matter and not of form. But it is division of gold, not just division of the matter which is at present gold, without dividing the gold. Yet the parts into which gold divides are still gold: that is why gold is capable of ' becoming many '. But, it may be replied, the *whole* of gold is in each of the divisions. We should not say that: that is the absurd formula ' exists in its entirety apart from itself ' which Plato construct-ed, and which so well characterises the *universalia in rebus* theory. ' The whole of gold ' should mean ' all the gold there is ', and that is *not* in each of the divisions. But the whole of what ' gold ' means is in each of the divisions!—That means that the whole of the *definition* of gold applies to each of the divisions, and that is true.

With an organised substance like a plant or an animal, division does not usually produce two things each of which is still the plant or animal in question. However, the whole stock can be conceived as one lump which has suffered division, on the following analogy: let our initial lump of gold be a certain shape, and let it always be growing in extent by putting out excrescences of the same shape, which then break off; and let ' a gold ' mean the whole of such a definitely shaped nodule of gold. Then if *a* gold is divided, the separated parts will not usually be golds, just as separated parts of animals are not usually animals; but the basic principle by which the form ' is divided and becomes many ' is not different from what it was for the plain lump.

The sense in which the individual is not the same as the form is that the name of the individual is connected with an identifiable bit of matter, since at any given time we can indicate the matter of the individual existing at that time. Socrates and Plato, then, or this lump of gold and that are the same substance, in the sense that the answer to the question ' what are they? ' is the same—' humans ' or ' gold '; and they are different substances in the sense that they are different (and separated) segments of the total mass of stuff that is alive with human life, or that is gold, at a given time.

Aristotle, we have seen, raises the question ' Is each individual man, say, the same as his *what he is*? ' and gives a (qualified) affirma-

tive answer to it. Now the question may seem to contain an infringe-
ment of the very rule I have used in explaining Aristotle's ' substances ', first and second: I mean the rule that things cannot be the
same without qualification. If we are asked 'Are X and Y the same? '
we can ask ' the same what? ' and we ought to ask this if the context
does not make it clear what the answer is: if there is no answer in
a given context the question fails to have a good sense. That may well
seem to be the case here (I owe the point to Professor W. C. Kneale).
But the answer in this context is: ' the same substance '. Here it looks
as if one should ask ' the same first substance, or the same second
substance? ' on the grounds that since both have been introduced, the
term ' substance ', without qualification, is ambiguous.

Now if we try out these alternatives we get the following results:

(a) Socrates is the same first substance as (is indicated by the
expressions telling us) what he is.

(b) Socrates is the same second substance as (is expressed by the
expressions telling us) what he is.

In (b) the ' is ' must be the sign of the composition that constitutes a predicative sentence, and the whole sentence (b) is a generalisation of such sentences as ' Socrates is a man ', ' Socrates is an
animal '. Thus (b) gives us no theory beyond that of the *Categories*.
(a) expresses Aristotle's advanced theory as we have it in the *Metaphysics*. By contrast with (a), Socrates is not the same *per se* existent
as is indicated by the expressions telling us how he is, how big he is,
what he is doing or suffering, what his posture is, etc.

We see that Aristotle is not against our *ever* speaking of a relation
between a subject and what the predicate stands for. On the contrary,
when the predicate does signify a *per se* being in the sense we have
explained, but still is not a predication in the category of substance,
he holds that there is not an identity between the subject and what is
spoken of in the predicate, but that what is spoken of in the predicate
is something that exists *in* the subject, or that the subject *has*. These
expressions he regards as wholly inappropriate to what is signified
by the predicates in the category of substance. In the case of humanity, or animality, or the differentia that shews what kind of an animal
a man is, he would feel the same paradox about saying that the
subject *has* them as is expressed about the soul in the lines:

John has a soul;
Upon the whole
The tombstone lies that says: *hic jacet.*
But if John really has a soul,
Who in the world is John who has it?

His aim could be summed up, from a modern point of view, as that of characterising what is expressed by the quite special type of predication in which the predicate (supposedly) tells us what the subject is. We say ' There is an x such that x is a dog and x is white and x barks '; now the different status of ' dog ' among these predicates can be brought out by considering that, ' There is an x such that x is first white and then not white ' (' first barks and then does not bark ') raises no problems; but ' There is an x such that x is first a dog and then not a dog ' should prompt us to ask ' What, then, is the x that is first a dog and then not a dog? '

The second phrase that I mentioned, composed of the definite article, the question ' what is it? ' and the infinitive of the verb ' to be ', I render as ' the *what-is-it* to be that ' (or ' the what it is to be that ') of a thing. The expression is uncouth, but not much more so than such an expression is in Greek. It is designed to refer to being such-and-such when ' such-and-such ' is the name of a substance.

But just as ' what? ' has a wider as well as a more restricted sense, so this phrase too can get applied to being such-and-such where ' such-and-such ' is a quality, relation, etc. It is as if Aristotle were struggling to characterise a type of reference which was only guaranteed by the way in which the words signifying in different categories were actually used; when he arrives at an expression for this, he finds he cannot forbid its application beyond what it was first devised for; but, he says, this is its *primary* application. If we start by distinguishing between *what* things are and (the various kinds of) *how* they are, we find that we want to speak of *what* (such-and-such a case of) *how* they are is. E.g. *What* Socrates is, is a *man*; *how* he is, is *in good health;* but may we not want to say *what* health is? (cf. *Met.* Z 1031 a 8–14).

It should now be clear how unfortunate and unilluminating it is to use the word ' essence ', with the suggestions it bears nowadays, in describing Aristotle's doctrine of *per se* and *per accidens* existents. The essence of a thing would seem to be constituted by any characteristics that it necessarily has; now if we think this is useful in explaining Aristotle we shall run into serious difficulties. It will go with explaining ' accidental ' only as ' non-essential ', and this in turn, as ' non-necessary '.

Now it is true that Aristotle explains the accidental as the non-necessary, and that predicates belonging to the ' what it is to be that ' of a thing are necessary; but that does not justify us in identifying the latter with necessary predicates; for he does not hold that all necessary predicates enter into the definition. This would be suggested by the identification of the accidental with the non-essential. But this leaves out another class of predicates which Aristotle mentions, the *propria* or peculiar predicates, i.e. such as are predicated convertibly of a thing or kind, but do not belong to its definition. By Aristotle's conception of necessity, if anything is always true it is necessary. The peculiar predicates of a kind will, then, be certain necessary, non-accidental, predicates which do not belong to the definition.[1]

So much is fairly familiar ground. But what happens if we try to bring this theory into connexion with the doctrine of *per se* and *per accidens* existence which we have been examining? This doctrine gives us only a single division: an existence must be either *per se* or *per accidens*, when a true predication determines an existence. If, then, what is *per accidens* is non-necessary, it looks as if, where ' ϕ ' is a peculiar predicate and ' a ' the name of a substantial kind, ' ϕa ' must signify a *per se* existent. But that cannot be true in the sense we have discussed except where ϕ belongs to the definition. In all other cases, where the predication, if true, signifies an existent, ' ϕa ' must signify a *per accidens* existent. In connexion with *per accidens*

---

[1] There is obviously room for another class of predicates, namely ones which are always true of a certain kind, but do not belong in the definition and are not true only of that kind. Why does Aristotle not admit such a class? Suppose that all A's are naturally B, but many other kinds are B too. Then in one sense, a B may or may not be an A. Aristotle may have inferred from this that an A need not always be a B (cf. *An. Pr.* 25b17). These questions can only be solved by a full understanding of Aristotle's ideas about necessity; but we have not got this, and we know they were not all coherent. The statement that if anything is always true it is necessary is equivalent to the statement that if it is not necessary it is not always true, and this in turn to the statement that if it is possible for it not to be true then at some time it is not true. Aristotle held all these positions, as that if anything is possible it must happen sometime; but it is not clear what restrictions would result from a correct interpretation of this, e.g. whether this commits him to a belief in the golden mountain's coming to be at some time. Cf. Mr. J. Hintikka's ' *Necessity, Universality and Time in Aristotle* ', Ajatus XX. 1957.

existents, then, the association between '*per accidens*' and 'non-necessary' is broken, and if one does not notice this, one will find Aristotle's whole theory plunged in inextricable confusion. That association is broken when Aristotle, directly referring to the categories, develops his theory of *per se* and *per accidens* existents.

In his dictionary of expressions in Metaphysics *Δ*, Aristotle considers other meanings of '*per se*'. One application it has, he says, is the one we have been discussing, namely that the 'what-is-it to be that' of a thing is said of it *per se*. But another is, that the first recipient of a characteristic A, is said to be A *per se* whether that first recipient is the thing itself that has the characteristic, or is something in it. E.g. when a thing is white, the 'first recipient' of the characteristic is its surface, so the surface is said to be *per se* white. It is hardly necessary to say that this does not mean that surfaces, or white surfaces, have to be white, or are essentially white, or are permanently white!

To understand what Aristotle means by 'the first recipient', we have to remember something that we have already touched on: namely that the pseudo-concept 'object' cannot be used to supply the place of the general term 'A' in the expression 'the same A', which we use when we say that, e.g., 'The same A has properties B and C' or 'is first B and then C'. Let something be both white and square. Nowadays we speak of an x such that x is white and x is square. The 'first recipient' of these qualifications will be shown by the first general term A at which it is possible to stop in seeking *what* it is that is both white and square. E.g., if the same thing is both white and square, then this is perhaps because the same *surface* is both white and square. Thus, the surface is the 'first recipient' of e.g., the qualification 'white', and Aristotle says that this is one sense of being such-and-such *per se*. In this sense, presumably a man will be *per se* educated and so a science of education will treat of men, as a science concerned with whiteness will treat of surfaces. For the most interesting contention made in connexion with beings *per accidens*, namely, that there can be no science of them, relates to beings which are not *per se* even in *this* sense. There is no science, for example, dealing with the educated white (and hence, we may say, with the education of white men) though there will be one of *education of men*, this being *per se*. Similarly, we cannot look scientifically for causes of beings *per accidens*—i.e. for a general theory of crime or

' delinquency ' for example, for delinquency, being a habit of acting contrary to the laws of the community in which one finds oneself, would unlike, say, vice and virtue be a good example of a being *per accidens*. Any Aristotelian ' principle of causality ' would be severely restricted in its range of application. Coincidences do not have causes which are the subjects of a science.

In these connexions, Aristotle makes some very difficult remarks which illumine his views on definition and ' the what-is-it to be that ' of things. He does not regard as a definition any and every form of words that tells us the meaning of a given name. If that were a definition, he remarks, then the Iliad would be a definition—i.e., you would be giving a definition of the title (or presumably of any phrase referring to the poem) by reciting the whole poem. Presumably any significant form of words can be given an explanation by means of other words; but such an explanation is not therefore a definition. It is clear that Aristotle thinks that for a definition there has to be something to define; not merely a form of words to explain. Nor is there necessarily something to define, because a given form of words has an application: for example, he does not think that a white man is an object of definition, though of course the expression ' white man ' has application, since there are white men.

He arrives at these views in the following way: the ' what-is-it to be that ' of a thing is given by what is said of it *per se*. But it is not just anything that is said of it *per se*, because ' white ' is said *per se* of a surface, but does not give the ' what-is-it to be that ' of a surface. If it did, he says, then being a surface would be the same thing as being white.

Here we must once again emphasize that Aristotle does *not* mean that ' being a surface ' would *mean* the same thing as ' being white '. For we can see that he must hold that being an animal is the same thing as being a man, when the animal in question is a man, but still the expressions ' being an animal ' and ' being a man ' do not mean the same and he did not think they did. On the contrary: the account of the genus fits the species, but not vice versa. Rather, for there to be an animal is the very same thing as for there to be a man when the animal concerned is a man; it is not a supervenient existence, in something that is already an animal, to be a man. Thus what he is denying, in the case where we have a white surface, is not that ' being a surface ' and ' being white ' have the same meaning, but that for

E

there to be this surface and for there to be this white are the same thing. This could easily be shewn in cases where this surface could cease to be white and still be the same surface.

Another Aristotelian expression that is constantly translated by 'essence' is an expression that in ordinary Greek would mean 'what is A' (ὅπερ A). To understand this, we have once again to remember Platonism, according to which a good man, for example, *participates* in what is good and it is wrong to say that he *is* good without understanding that this signifies only participation. What *is* good is what *good* is, what the word 'good' stands for. Now Aristotle retains the notion of 'being what *is* A', or 'what A is', because there are cases in which he thinks there is a contrast, and other cases in which he thinks there is no contrast, between *being A* and *being what is A* or *being what A is*. He even retains the notion of participation (in the *Topics*), but restricts it to the cases where there is *no* contrast between being A and being what *is* A. Where we have a genus and a species the species participates in the genus, and this means that the definition of the genus applies to the species—and, we may add, remembering the *Categories*, to the individuals of the species. On the other hand, snow is white, but it is not *what is white* (or *what white is*) and that is why 'white' is not a genus of which snow is a species.

Thus Aristotle holds that a large range of predicates, but not all predicates, when truly predicated, stand for entities. Of these predicates, some stand for the very entity that is the subject of a singular proposition in which the predicate is truly predicated. These are predicates in the category of substance: genus, differentia, or species. Others do not stand for that entity though they may be predicated of it; and if the predications are true the entities they stand for are said to *exist in* the subject, or to be *had by* it. These entities are what were later called the 'accidents'. Both these types of entity are said to 'be *per se*'; but the expression formed by combining the subject name with a predicate signifying an entity other than the subject is allocated to describing 'being *per accidens*' and not 'being *per se*', and this is said strictly speaking not to have a definition: an example would be 'white Callias', or again 'a white man'.

This theory does not concern all general terms. For example, Aristotle denies that there is any such thing at all as "what is one'; or again 'what is being (existent)' or 'what is good'—in the sense that is, in which 'what is A' is an entity (existing in a subject or as a substance) that the predicate 'A' stands for. Further, very many terms—e.g. 'house', 'threshold'—have as part of their meaning a special position or arrangement, and perhaps even a purpose in the position or arrangement. The predicative copula in propositions with such predicates certainly expresses that something is true of the subject, but the passage from this to the predicate's signifying a *per se* existent is not permissible.

Part of the interest of Aristotle's doctrine lies in the way that he connected it with the 'principle of contradiction'. A long, difficult and bad-tempered passage in *Metaphysics Γ* makes this connexion.

Here we must note that for Aristotle the notion of propositional contradiction hardly existed. He does indeed sometimes speak of 'thus and not thus', which sounds like propositional contradiction; but his detailed treatment concerns a subject (a substance) and the impossibility of the same thing's holding and not holding of it; or of contraries' holding of it.

Aristotle says that this 'strongest of all principles' cannot be proved to someone who denies it, except by way of refutation—if he will only commit himself to 'signifying something'. He does not have to assert that something exists or does not exist; but only to signify something, both to himself and to someone else.

From what he goes on to say, it seems that what he wants is the utterance of a significant name. For, he says, the first thing that is clear is that the name signifies being or not being such-and-such. That is, it is still open to a man—so far as the argument has gone— to say that something can both be and not be such-and-such, but at least there is something definite that he would be saying it was and was not; so we are not in a state of complete flux and vagueness: not everything is a matter just of 'thus and not thus' (this is presumably a reference to Plato's *Theaetetus*).

He goes on further to suppose that the name uttered has been that of some 'per se existent': the example he takes is 'man'. It must, he says, have *one* meaning; for if it has many we must simply choose one: the many meanings that it has must be such that we take one of them, and not have subdivisions *ad infinitum*. If one could have subdivision *ad infinitum*, there would be no discussion possible between people. That is to say, definiteness of sense is essential to communication, and units of meaning are essential to definiteness of sense. It must be possible to deny just what someone else has said; otherwise there can be no discussion. This brings out the point of saying that the name signifies being or not being such-and-such. If someone uses the word ' red ' to say that something is red, and I to say it is not, then if we are communicating we must be meaning the same by ' red '. This point holds without prejudice to the question whether both may not be correct; granted this, there can be discourse, without it not, and if a man won't commit himself even to this, then he's no better than a cabbage! Aristotle evidently had some very irritating people to argue with.

His explanation of ' signifying one thing ', however, actually seems to bring in the whole theory we have been considering. That which is to signify one thing is evidently a general term: his example is ' man '. Let us put 'A' as the term used, and suppose that ' $\phi\chi$ ' is the definition of this term 'A'. Then, Aristotle says, 'A' is a term signifying one thing if and only if, given that A is anything, its being A is (being) $\phi\chi$ (Met. Γ 1006 a 34). And here, as I shall argue, ' being A' and ' being $\phi\chi$ ' have that technical sense which we have spent so much effort in elucidating.

One difficulty in understanding these clauses is that 'A' evidently stands in them as a *subject* which is an *unquantified general term*. But such subjects are not foreign to Aristotle. If a man is white, that is for him *man's* being white. Thus ' man is white ' and ' man is not white ' can both be true together: it is only when we introduce quantifiers (as we should now say) that we can form contradictories of this kind that cannot both be true. This at any rate is the doctrine of the *De Interpretatione*.

Aristotle proceeds to argue: if, given that 'A' = ' $\phi\chi$ ' being A is being $\phi\chi$, then it is impossible that ' being A ' should signify what ' not being A' signifies. He cannot be arguing that ' being A ' and ' not being A' will not have the *same sense*, for that is presupposed by the enquiry. He is not opposing people who say that to say ' is A ' and ' is not A' is to say just the same thing, but ones who say that these two different things may both hold of the same, just as ' white ' and ' educated ', which are different, may both hold of the same thing.

His argument presupposes that *if* ' being A' could signify what ' not being A' signified, then there would be nothing being which was being A when A was anything—i.e. when an A was the subject of some true predication. Can we supply an example? I think we can, if we consider ' being large '. Being two foot long might be being large, and might also be not being large. So ' being large ' can signify something that ' not being large ' also can signify. It follows that if a large thing is two foot long, its being large would not be being two foot long. This would shew that ' being large ' does *not* ' signify one thing '—i.e. that the expression ' being large ' is not itself the sign of a *per se* existent.

' Signifying the same,' then, does not mean ' having the same sense,' nor yet, he insists, does it mean ' holding of the same '. It begins to look as if his sense of ' signifying ' is *none* of those currently in use among present day and recent philosophers. His argument goes: if ' being A' does not signify what ' not being A' signifies, then 'A' as a predicate cannot signify what ' not A' as a predicate signifies. From this he infers that if it is *true* to call something 'A' it is *necessarily true* to say that it is $\phi\chi$. Therefore it *cannot* not be $\phi\chi$. Therefore it *cannot* be true to say it is not A.

This argument makes no sense except on the supposition that 'A' is a predicate in the category of substance, as is his actual example, ' man '. To see this, we need first to see that it must be a predicate indicating a *per se* existent.

' White ' and ' educated ', we may say, are different labels which may rightly hang on the same thing. So, the argument of Aristotle's opponents ran, why may not 'A' and ' not A', though they are different labels, rightly hang on the same thing? To this Aristotle's reply is: is there something definite which is being A? If not, it says nothing to label something 'A'. (An example of this could be given: it says nothing to hang the label ' good ' or ' one ' or ' existent' on something: this example, which is consonant with Aristotle's doctrine, shews that his ' principle of contradiction ' is not ' for all p, not both p and not-p ').

Now if the ' being A' which is something definite, namely $\phi\chi$, is what is signified by 'A' if there is an A (or, as Aristotle puts it, if there is anything that A is), and if ' signifying the same ' neither means having the same sense nor means holding of the same, then Aristotle's doctrine is only coherent on the supposition that by ' what " being A" signifies ' he means an entity indicated by the predicate 'A' when it is truly predicated of a singular subject. But this cannot be a *per accidens* existent, like a white man because ' white ' indicates

one particular and 'man' another, when 'white man' is truly
predicated of a singular subject. If this were not so, then the being a
man that we get when ' α is a white man ' is true would be the same
as the being white. Therefore 'A' is a predicate indicating a *per se*
existent.

Suppose, then, that this predicate were ' white ', which as we have
seen is a predicate indicating a *per se* existent of a kind that exists in
a subject: the white of this paper is such a *per se* existent. Now it is
true that the white of this paper is necessarily white, for any change
from being white here involves the-white-of-this-paper's ceasing to
exist.

Since this paper is white, there is a white (thing) of which various
other things are true. But the statement ' there is a white (thing) '
is ambiguous: does it refer to the *per se* existent, the white of this
paper, or to the paper? (*Met. Z.* 1031 b 23–5). If, then, we say ' whatever else the white (thing) is, $\phi\chi$ will necessarily hold of it ', we find
that this is not true; for ' the white thing ' may mean the paper. It is
only when 'A' is a predicate in the category of substance that something's being an A implies that the proposition stating that it is $\phi\chi$
is a necessary proposition. For, Aristotle says, (*Met. Γ* 1007 a 32)
though a man is white, he is not ' what is white ', i.e. he is not the
per se existent indicated by ' white ' in the true proposition stating
that he is white. Here we must notice that though we may speak of
that *per se* existent as being white, this is not because there is a white
which is *of* it—which is what is ordinarily meant by calling something
white: it is only that there is a white which it is. This helps to explain
Aristotle's reiterated objections to expressions like ' white white
man ', ' nose-hollowness of a nose ' which strike us as merely redundant. They would not be merely redundant but absurd if they
implied that there was a further white which was the white of the
white, which was the white of a man. If a brush is the tail of a fox,
we must not construe ' fox's brush ' as meaning ' tail of a fox of a
fox '; that, apparently, is how Aristotle would have construed it.

An actual interlocutor, who was acquainted with Aristotle's views
and was obeying his invitation to pronounce a word that signified
something both to himself and others, might have pulled Aristotle's
leg by saying ' one ' or ' good '. For as we have seen, Aristotle needs
a particular kind of name; according to his own teaching the words
' one ', ' good ', ' existent ' would not qualify as words ' signifying

one thing'. This apparently innocent demand covers a special requirement, and the use of 'signifying one thing' is a peculiar and technical one.

He explicitly links the discussion of his form of the principle of contradiction with his account of substance: people who deny the principle of contradiction have to deny substance: that is, they have to deny that there is any such thing as 'what it is to be man' or 'what it is to be an animal'. For these phrases give us what it is to be a given individual: if both what is expressed by them and by their negations could be found in an individual, what it is to be that individual would not be expressed by them. Thus, I should interpret the argument, Aristotle's principle of contradiction holds at any rate for predicates such that being the same X is being the same individual, and people who deny the principle have to deny that there is any such thing, and maintain that every predicate attaches accidentally.

The interest of this argument is heightened by the fact that this *would* most commonly be maintained among English-speaking philosophers at the present day who would reject altogether the concepts of 'real definition', Aristotelian form, and essence, taking all these to be roughly equivalent. But we should notice that 'essence' is not really a notion of Aristotle's, and there is not even any place for it in his thought, though it was developed in later Aristotelian philosophy, which distinguished between 'essence' and 'form'. Popularly 'essence' has always seemed easier to understand then 'form'. Yet in general we form abstract nouns (e.g. 'caninity') corresponding to substantial predicates much less readily and naturally than ones corresponding to other predicates. Such formations do not occur in Aristotle, who has simply 'form', 'matter' and 'substance' which last may be understood as matter, as form, as genus, or as the individual composed of matter and form, and no notion of 'essence' or 'nature', which is a kind of universal *man* or *humanity*. As Locke remarked, 'humanity' in its ordinary use is not related to 'man' as 'whiteness' is to 'white'.

We can now get an insight into the contention of the *Metaphysics* that strictly speaking only substances have definitions. A definition must always be in other terms, and be such that the being A, where 'A' is the defined term, is the very individual that is indicated by 'being ϕ' and 'being χ' where the definition is '$\phi\chi$'. With the (doubtful) exception of mathematicals, only the names of substantial kinds are susceptible of this kind of definition: terms do not in general combine except to form expressions indicating *per accidens* existents.

There appears to be a confusion in Aristotle between: ' Necessarily (if p, then not-not-p), ' and ' If p, then necessarily (not-not-p) '. For his considerations about ' being A' relate to the latter proposition and only have significant consequences where 'A' is a predicate in the category of substance. But the argument is apparently also directed against people who, as it seems, denied the former proposition. It seems that these people said: ' Given that a is A, still it is possibly also at the same time not A', supporting this with the highly sophistical argument that if a is also C, and ' C ' means something different from 'A' then a is [something that is] not A. Aristotle does not wholly reject this argument, but replies that a is then not A in an accidental and irrelevant sense. Assuming him to be right in his contention that, where p is a true singular substantial predication it is a necessary proposition, the relation between this fact and the principle of contradiction in the form ' For all p, necessarily (if p, then not-not-p) ' needs to be sorted out, with due attention to the placing of the modal operators and of the expression 'at the same time' in the various propositions that come up for consideration. This Aristotle did not do, so the connexion between his thesis about true singular substantial predication and the principle of contradiction in its most familiar form remains obscure. We may conclude that the ' principle of contradiction ', as effectively discussed by him, is not the principle we are familiar with, but is rather: ' If ϕa, " ϕ " being a predicate in the category of substance, then " $\sim \phi a$ " is an impossible proposition '.

The futility of not accepting the principle of contradiction—at least where the sense of an expression is definite—is so evident that we are little inclined to discuss the matter. But may not this be the heart of the matter—where the sense is definite? Nowadays we define ' not-p ' as *the* proposition that is true when p is false and false when p is true. But this raises the question how we know that there always is such a proposition, and only one such proposition. Further, this is propositional contradiction; what are we to say about predicate contradiction? What we in fact do in logic is to *postulate a non-empty domain of discourse*, and allocate to certain signs—say small letters at the beginning of our alphabet—the role of names of individuals. Having so set the stage, we can say that ' $\sim \phi a$ ' is *the* negation of ϕa, *the* proposition that is true when ϕa is false and false when ϕa is true. To say *what a* was in a given case would take us outside the *domain of discourse*.

Now does not the supposition ' this is a non-empty domain of discourse ' imply that there is such a thing as *what a* is? Yet no proposition ' ϕa ' within the theory that is being set forth could say what *a* is; for we do not, as far as I know, have theories in which there are predicates ϕ such that ' $\sim \phi a$ ' though well-formed is excluded on grounds of *what a* is; if ' ϕa ' is excluded as false this is because it has been found out that ϕ does not hold of *a*; but if ϕ expressed *what a* was, then it could not be *found out* that $\sim \phi$ did not hold of *a*—since the supposition that it did would be the supposition that there was no such thing as *a* for anything to hold or not hold of. Or if it can be ' found out ', this could only be because the sign ' *a* ' had been only partially understood.

Aristotle's substance-predicates and definitions express what the designata of names of individuals are.

There is thus a comparison and a contrast with Wittgenstein of the *Tractatus*. For Wittgenstein also thought that there had to be *what* the objects named in propositions are, but that this could not be expressed by any proposition; propositions, he says, *can* only express how things are, not what they are. And he uses the word ' substance ' of his objects: they ' form the substance of the world' ; the requirement that names of them should be possible is the requirement of definiteness of sense, without which there would not be that understanding of the sense of propositions which enables us to draw conclusions from them.

Wittgenstein's substance differs from Aristotle's in being simple, permanent, inexpressible—and chimerical. But if there were a proposition saying what an object (or substance) was, then it is clear that it would be of a very different character from any propositions stating what, as it happens (whether it happens necessarily or not) holds of a given substance. This consideration may help someone versed in modern philosophy to view with a more understanding eye the quite special position that Aristotle gives to propositions stating the ' what ' of his substances. Aristotle's (material) substances, by contrast with Wittgenstein's ' objects ', are complex, generable and corruptible, expressible and non-chimerical. It is natural that his doctrine of them should be far from the beautiful simplicities of the *Tractatus*.

The fact that the ' what ' of substances is something that can be investigated and discovered is the root of the distinction between nominal and real definition. Armed with a nominal definition—say of a unicorn—one could set out to discover whether there existed such a thing; only when its existence was established could one make a biological investigation that would determine the real definition of the species. But Aristotle's conception of ' scientific demonstration ', in so far as he has a general theoretical account of this, is *a priori* and fantastic, being infected by the conviction he held (mentioned at the beginning of this essay) that in elucidating categorical syllogism be had discovered a key to the nature of ' scientific knowledge '.

Let us return to the quite special character that he assigns to statements in which a predicate belonging to the category of substance is predicated of an individual. We have seen that he wants to say that the individual is its *what-is-it to be that*, which is indicated by such predicates. The reason for this is that he does not want to have the individual standing in a relation to what is indicated by the predicate.

On the other hand, he was in great difficulties at this point. For he could not hold that the individual was identical with its *what-is-it to be that* in such a sense as to make individuals of the same species identical with one another. His solution was to say that they were identical in species or kind but different in matter.

The familiar expressions ' numerically the same ', ' numerically different ', etc., seem to originate with Aristotle. At any rate as used at the present day they are bad expressions, because they suggest that counting of itself implies that individuals and not kinds are being counted. ' Numerically different ' as opposed to ' specifically different ' or ' qualitatively different ' is a mere label: we are adverting to a kind of difference in counting contained in the different ways one may count letters on a page (' tokens ' or ' types '). But while ' specifically different ' is genuinely explanatory, ' numerically different ', which has an air of being explanatory, is not so at all: it is a mere, as opposed to a suitable, label. A genuinely explanatory label here is ' materially different ' as opposed to ' specifically different '. Thus before we can grasp Aristotle's theory of substantial predication, we must consider the notions of matter and form.

The concept of matter here introduced is not any kind of hypo-thesis. It is that very notion of matter, or stuff, which we employ when we ask e.g. whether a certain chemical change takes place with or without the addition or loss of any matter. We test this e.g. by the use of sealed vessels, or by apparatus designed to shew whether when e.g. two substances combine to form a third, any gas is given off.

The origin of the notion of matter, then, is to be found in con-siderations about substantial change. Matter, Aristotle says, has to be understood in what changes; now with some changes we can say what the thing that changes is during the whole time in which it is changing. E.g. if something changes its place or its shape or its colour, we can say that it is a particular man, or lump of plastic material, or apple that changes. Or if bricks and mortar, etc., become a house by being put together to make one we can say that such-and-such bricks and mortar, remaining such, become a house. In all these cases the matter of the change is the nameable and characteris-able object or objects that are the subject of change.

The Greek natural philosophers, according to Aristotle, held that all change was of this character: that is to say that whatever changes take place one can ask concerning the subject of change: ' What is it *all* the time? '—and the ultimate answer to this question, which holds regardless of what change is involved, will tell us the permanent elements of things. Aristotle by contrast held that in the case of substantial change, since the name of a (' second ') substance told one what a thing was, it is an error to think that there is any such thing as ' what this is all the time '. Hence, he says, matter, as such, is neither of any kind nor of any particular quantity, nor any-thing else, nor on the other hand do the negations of any of these things apply to it. For if some given matter were as such, say, water, or a pint, then it could not cease to be water when water undergoes a substantial change, nor cease to be a pint when there is expansion or contraction; nor do the negations apply to the matter as such, because if the matter as such were not-water, or not-a-pint, then it could not ever be water, or ever be a pint in volume. But a certain parcel of matter may become water (from having been something else) in substantial change, or become a pint (from having been more or less) when there is contraction or expansion. Of course matter never exists except in one form or another.

We may be able to identify bits of matter for a time, even for a very long time; but it does not follow that a once identifiable bit of matter must remain (theoretically) identifiable. If I force a glass of water into a large bottle of water, without allowing the escape of air, then I can say with fair confidence that the stuff in the bottle now includes the stuff that was in the bottle before, plus the stuff that was in the glass; and I may have reason to say that the water in the bottle is wholly the same stuff as the water in the bottle before plus the water that was in the glass before. But is it necessarily the case that I could theoretically identify the stuff that was in the glass, beyond saying that it is now part and parcel of the water that is now in the bottle? It may be that I could always devise some way of marking it off, so that it remains identifiable. But it is one thing merely to label something, and another to give it a special character by which to recognise it; and it is not clear that every case of giving it a special character by which to recognise it is always like a scratch we might put on a chair, a mere mark: it is not off-hand clear that we do not thereby *give* it an identity capable of persisting in circumstances in which it would otherwise have been lost. At any rate, Aristotle's conception of matter allows for this possibility; for Aristotle the identifiable must always have *some* determinate character, and every determinate character of material things is alterable.

This is not to say that every time Aristotle speaks of matter he is speaking of what is absolutely indeterminate. On the contrary; whenever we can say what a given thing is made of—as, e.g., that a bronze is made of bronze, or that a syllable is composed of its letters —what it is made of is its matter.

We know from Plato's *Theaetetus* of the existence in Greek philosophy of a logical, as opposed to a merely physical, theory of elements. In the theory sketchily described by Plato, speech is a network of names, which are the names of simple objects: these can only be named and not defined; we and everything else are com-pounded out of these simple objects. The *Metaphysics* shews that Aristotle gave a good deal of consideration to this theory; he rejected it on the ground that when the compound ceases to exist, the elements are still there; there must therefore be something about the com-pound, beyond the elements, which is not itself a further element, but through which the elements form the compound. Thus where there are identifiable elements, these are only the matter of the thing in which they are elements, and any theory is inadequate which treats the elements as the whole story.

It is very natural, if once one has adopted the idea of 'elements', to think that what needs to be spoken of in addition is the way the elements are combined or arranged. In some cases, e.g. in that of the written syllable, this is what we want; the arrangement of the letters forms the syllable. But the syllable is not formed from the letters and the arrangement; rather it is formed from the letters by the arrangement. Here we see one of the Aristotelian 'causes': for that through which the elements yield the syllable is the cause of the syllable; and this Aristotle calls the 'formal cause'. What the compound is formed from, the matter, is by contrast called the material cause. Thus, in expounding Aristotle's theory of material substances, we should use the expression 'composed of form and matter' only with the greatest caution, commonplaces of Aristotelian philosophy as such expressions are; for the expression 'composed of' properly relates only to the matter.

The form, then, is what makes what a thing is made *of* into that thing. It may be literally a shape, as it is the shape that makes bronze into a statue; or again an arrangement, e.g. of letters to make a syllable; or a position, as the position of a beam makes it a threshold or lintel; or a time, as the time of eating food makes that food breakfast.

In all these cases, and a host of others which could be cited, the idea of the formal cause is readily intelligible, because the matter which the formal cause makes to be a statue, or a syllable, or a lintel, or breakfast, strikes us as something already having a fully actual existence on its own account. The same bronze in another shape might be an urn, the same food eaten at another time might be dinner the same letters in another arrangement a different syllable, the same beam another part of a house, or part of a different structure. Yet this can be paralleled by the fact that the same stuff may be now wine, now vinegar. What really distinguishes some of those other cases from this one is that the same food might be merely in a cupboard, without being any definite meal at all, the same letters might not be arranged to form a syllable at all, and the same beam no part of any structure.

The bronze of the statue is an exception here, for so long as it is identifiable as that (parcel of) bronze it is in some shape, or in various bits each of some shape or other. (Note that I use a slightly awkward expression to say what I mean here, because the normal way of putting it: ' identifiable as the very same matter ', is *derived* from Aristotelian philosophy.) Thus this bronze as such is not of any given shape. What are we to say of it? It can be identified, since we can say that this bronze statue is (materially) the same bronze as a bronze sphere from which it was cast. But without any shape it does not exist. Yet we cannot say that what first has this and then that shape is nothing. Here Aristotle uses the idea of potentiality: the bronze that *can* have this shape is a potential existent, and in the actual bronze sphere or statue we have to discern the potential existent, which is actualised by, say, the spherical shape it has now.

The contrast with the case of the letters is evident; for they perhaps already actually exist, unformed into any syllable. They might, let us suppose, be cut out letters in a box, a plaything for a child, which when placed together in a certain order make up a syllable.

The idea of an element in a Greek idea: the Greek word for ' element ' is the word for a letter of the alphabet, as indeed is the Latin word ' elementum ' (perhaps LMN-tum). Now an element in the sense of a letter exists in its compound, the syllable, not just as something that is made actual by being in the compound: it is something actual on its own account in the compound apart from the fact of its being in the compound. And similarly with the beam that makes the lintel or the food that makes breakfast.

The matter of a natural substance is like the bronze of the statue in this regard; it will no doubt have been for this reason that ' shape ', *morphe*, is one of the words that Aristotle uses, in an extended sense, for the ' cause ' that makes stuff to be, say water or wine, as the time of eating makes the food breakfast or the position in the structure makes the beam a lintel. The other word that he employs for this notion is *eidos*. In origin, like *idea* (which is the word Aristotle uses when he wants to speak of *Platonic* forms) this word means the look of a thing; but in ordinary usage it also had the sense ' kind '. (The Latin word *species* has the same sense history.)

The bronze of the statue, which is actualised in respect of shape by the shape that makes it into this statue, is already actual in respect of other properties—e.g. those that make it to be bronze. Since the shape is the formal cause of the statue, and the bronze is what immediately received the shape, the bronze is the immediate or proximate matter of the statue.

Aristotle's notion of matter, as that out of which something is formed, covers both the contemporaneously discernible *stuff of which it is made*, such as the bronze of the statue, and the previously discernible *stuff out of which it has come*. E.g. he thinks of water as the matter of water vapour (though he does not think that water vapour *is* water) because water vapour comes from water.

Yet he does not hold that in every case where a substance A changes into a substance B, it is correct to say that A is the matter of B, or that A is potentially B. It looks as if where B strikes him as a degeneration from A, he wishes only to say that the *stuff* that is actually A is potentially B. Thus when wine turns into vinegar, and a living animal becomes a dead body, he denies that wine is the matter of vinegar, and that the animal is potentially the corpse. The reason that he mentions is the irreversability of the change. Wine turns into vinegar, but vinegar does not turn into wine unless by turning into water, with which for example one might water a vine (we should remember in connexion with this example that, to all appearances, if you keep wine long enough it simply turns into vinegar, and if you keep the vinegar long enough it simply turns into water); and the dead body does not become a live animal again except by first becoming the matter from which the live animal is formed; for example, by the process of digestion on the part of an animal that eats the flesh of the dead body.

Thus, I suppose, *if* we could turn graphite into charcoal and charcoal into diamonds, but could not get charcoal out of diamonds again without first turning the diamonds into graphite, Aristotle would say that the graphite was the matter of both charcoal and diamonds and was potentially charcoal and diamonds; but that charcoal was not itself the matter of diamonds nor potentially diamonds—diamonds would be what the matter of charcoal turned into. But, supposing that the only way of getting diamonds from graphite was first to turn the graphite into charcoal, it would be impossible to give any grounds—so far as concerns reversability of change—for regarding graphite as the matter of charcoal and diamonds rather than for regarding diamonds as the matter of charcoal and graphite. Now presumably Aristotle would have thought that the only way of turning water into vinegar was first to turn it into wine and then to let the wine corrupt.

Is he not influenced by a feeling that wine is better than vinegar?

In my imaginary parallel I deliberately assigned to diamonds the place of vinegar in the parallel process—but would not Aristotle have been inclined to give diamonds the ' best ' position? The generation of one substance is the corruption of another, but he clearly thinks that not all cases are on a par; he feels that the generation of wine from the water with which the vine is watered is *really* generation from *water as the matter* of the change; while that of vinegar from wine is only *per accidens* generation from the wine—because the wine is not matter receiving a *higher* form, but rather something of a lower form is generated, and so the matter here is really only the original matter of the wine, viz water.

There are, however, two readily intelligible considerations here. First, water is, as people say, a very common ' constituent' of things; and, second, we could understand someone's saying that there is more to wine (or to vinegar) than to water. (This even makes sense in terms of present day chemistry; water is less structurally compli- cated.) For Aristotle, of course, water was one of the four ' elements ' of archaic science: earth, water, air and fire. I think it helps us to have a slightly better appreciation of this if we think of it as if it meant: solid (*the* solid stuff), liquid (*the* liquid stuff), gas and fire. The familiar substances of everyday life would be formed by the mixture, compacting, or other organisation of these elements, whose completely pure state would perhaps be a postulated ideal possibility rather than anything actual. (Though fire is said to be the element that actually exists in the purest state.) According to Aristotle's own conceptions, however, there would be no impossibility about one ' element's ' turning into another: as we have seen he denies that there is anything that changeable things have to be all the time; water can turn into ' air '. For him, then, the ' elements ' would be the first *substantially characterisable* matter of substantially changeable things; and he will call the characteristic materials out of which highly organised substances are formed their ' matter ' only when the change strikes him as a change to what is better, is more highly organised, has more to it. Further he holds that the four elements themselves are not on a level; earth is the most material, and fire the element that has most to it, ' more form and substance '. ' Prime matter ' is the *substantially uncharacterisable* stuff of a change from being one to being another element. It is not in itself intelligible, but has to be understood as what is capable of this change; for there is nothing to it but the capacity of being now of this, now of that substantial kind. That is not to say that the *concept* of matter is an unintelligible one; on the contrary, it is, Aristotle says, clear or obvious; the *concept* of form is far more difficult to understand. But the material aspect of a thing cannot be spoken of at all without characterising it somehow—e.g. we can speak of the matter of a statue because it is bronze, i.e. matter already in the form of bronze. 'The form can be spoken of, and anything can be spoken of *qua* having a form, but the material aspect as such, never'. (*Met.* Z 1035 a 7–9.) We might say: 'But is it not being spoken of, when it is called the material aspect?' It is; but Aristotle's point is that there is no answer to the question what this material aspect is; for you say what something is precisely by giving its form. One gives a form by saying 'bronze' or 'flesh and bone'.

Let us return to the letters and the syllable. In calling the letters the matter of the syllable I made them material letters—cut out plastic letters, for example, such as a child might play with. It is just for this reason that I was able to say that here the notion of the formal cause—the arrangement that makes these letters into a syllable—seemed rather easy to understand, since the 'matter' was something that had an independent existence. But it only 'had an independent existence' because it was already matter of a certain kind (plastic) formed into certain shapes. Now if I say that the syllable 'ab' is composed of the letters a and b put side by side in that order I am giving a complete definition of the syllable, but here I have not mentioned any matter, as I mentioned the matter of which a syllable might be composed when I spoke of the cut-out plastic letters.

Now suppose that certain plastic letters have been arranged to form the syllable. I give *these* plastic letters in this arrangement the proper name 'Jack', and say 'Jack is the syllable "ab"'. This is the sentence that Aristotle's theory suggests we compare to 'Socrates is a man'. The general term occurring as a predicate signifies only the form—the 'actuality'; this is predicated of the matter. (*Met.* H. 1043 a 6–7.) The proper name, at any one time at which its bearer exists, signifies a certain parcel of matter *qua* having this form. As for the (Platonic) form, *man, the horse, etc.*, which stand over against individuals, and are universals, these, Aristotle says, are not substances but are a sort of composite of the definition and 'this matter'

F

[impossibly] considered as universal. (*Met.* Z. 1035 b 28–31.) That is to say, such a ' form ' is a mere chimera; Aristotle has been ill served by his translators here, who have not perceived the evident fact that this sentence is another comment on Plato's theory of forms, and not an exposition of his own theory at all. The Latin translators also failed to notice this point; hence Aquinas too was misled into treating this as a part of Aristotle's own theory.

Now, very rarely, there is a special word for the Aristotelian form, as opposed to its being indicated by the way the substantial term signifies when it occurs predicatively. The paradigm case of this is ' soul '. I have perhaps put this tendentiously; it would be Aristotle's claim—for this is his explanation of the soul. Thus he would regard ' Socrates is a man ' as saying that such and such matter is informed with the human form, or lives with human life, has a human soul. But the matter is only identified as matter so informed; therefore our information comes to this: that a certain parcel of matter which has the human form has the human form. Which parcel of matter this was, in the case of Socrates as opposed to the case of Plato, could only be indicated by reference to the senses. Thus for Aristotle the difference between two contemporary things of the same kind is only difference of matter; their definitions are the same.

Aristotle is constantly insisting that the form (which we have now found to be what is signified by terms which belong to one or another of the categories, *when these terms occur predicatively*) is ' actuality '—when the form is substantial, i.e. when the predicate is in the category of substance, the form is ' substance and actuality '. Further, form alone is ' intelligible '. That is to say, only the words which express form enable us to pick out real existences, and what they express is what makes things be what they are; there is indeed such a thing as what in them is *made to be* what they are, but this is the matter, which cannot itself be characterised except as the possibility of being or becoming such and such.

Now the existence of the things is precisely the actualisation of this possibility: thus we find Aristotle constantly distinguishing between existence on the one hand and on the other (a) actuality (b) whatever it is that is actualised by that actuality. In comparison with the latter, existence seems to relate to form; the existence of the matter that composes Socrates is substantial existence as a human being; but in comparison with ' actuality ' or the formal cause, existence is particular and material. The contrast between actuality and existence is drawn especially in his theory of knowledge, according to which if, say, a sighted animal receives a sense impression of red, the ' actuality ' or ' form ' signified by the word ' red ' is one and the same in the seen object and the sensation, but the ' existence ' of the red thing and the sensation of red is different. Either existence, however, is the actualisation—and hence the actuality, and one and the same actuality—of what was before a mere potentiality. Similarly the intellect is actualised by the forms which also actualise matter; again, the ' actuality ' will be the same but the ' existence ' different.

The theory has the attraction of seeming to preserve that internal relation which must be shewn to hold between what we may quite generally style ' cognitions ' and their objects, without falling into idealism. The forms which actualise the intellect in understanding are without matter, and are made to be so by the intellect, which thus divides into a ' passive ' intellect actualised by these forms, and a ' productive ' intellect that makes the forms-without-matter: Aristotle compares this to light making colours actual. Thus it appears that the objects of understanding are only potential in material things, although, *as* they exist in material things, they are the actualisation of the matter of those things. It is ground for intense regret that Aristotle never expounded his ideas for the general public, shewing those unversed in these difficult conceptions how they might attain to them. For so far as his ideas are sound, they must be capable of a clearer exposition then he has given them.

It is a common error, dating, Sir David Ross tells us, from Plotinus, to suppose that Aristotle holds that all ' numerical difference ' is difference of matter. Aristotle's theory is that where there are many things of *the same species* coexistent then the difference is difference of matter; but a difference of kind would of itself be sufficient to account for numerical difference. It is important also to grasp that matter as the principle of individuation concerns only contemporaries. For living organisms at least, the identity over a period of time is determined by the persistence of the same form in continuously changing matter. If we imagine a pattern of light projected on to a conveyer belt, we can see that if ' X ', was the name of the pattern, and *an X* was a portion of the belt picked out by the pattern X, and if there were many Xs, then the contemporaneous X's would be distinguished from one another by being at any one time different portions of the belt, while an X at one time would be the same X as an X at another time because of the continuity of the pattern. This, then, is Aristotle's theory of the continuity of the individual in whom the matter changes over a period of time. He himself makes the comparison with a stretch of water marked off by a measure—new water keeps on flowing through. The human or other animal form takes the place of the measure that might be set up to mark off a mile of river (*De Gen. et Corr.*, I 5).

But the way in which the analogy is only an analogy, which cannot be pressed, is this: the matter of a substance e.g. of a living body, is in Aristotle's view in itself nothing but a potentiality: it is not e.g. actual flesh, blood and bones except *qua* informed by the human or other animal form, or life, or soul. Hence he says that the soul is the *what-it-is-to-be-a-body-of-that-kind*, and also calls it the actuality of the body. If the eye were itself an animal, and not just a part of an animal then, he says, sight would be its soul. This comparison, rightly understood, throws much light on his doctrine.

In the first place, why does he say: *if* the eye were an animal, i.e. if it existed on its own and not as a part, sight would be its soul? He is not making the simple comparison: as sight is to the eye, so the soul is to the body. For then there would be no need to say 'if the eye existed on its own'.

We are perhaps inclined to think of seeing as something that the eye—the ' vile jelly '—does or plays a part in; the eye's existence is prior to this, just as the existence of a machine consists in its being such and such an arrangement of parts, which, if set in motion in appropriate circumstances, effect such and such a result. That it was the purpose of the maker to produce what would effect such and such results is perhaps implicit in the concept of a machine, but this is extraneous to the machine's physical character and real existence. Or to use a simpler comparison, a knife cuts because it has a sharp edge and is used for cutting. But no one would think that the activity of cutting was the actualization of something which constituted the existence of what exists when there is a knife. *That* is, say, wood and steel of a certain shape and arrangement, and cutting is something that it is able to do because of the qualities of the steel and the shape and arrangement of the steel and wood. If the activity of cutting is in any sense the formal cause of the knife, this is because it is the final cause, the purpose we have in mind when we call this object a knife, and this final cause is part of our conception of a knife, so that what might very well exist, the same object, would not be a knife without it, e.g. if though it was like a knife it was designed for some other purpose. Its purpose is our interest in it, which is 'built into' the meaning of our term 'knife'. But the object's existence is neutral to such an interest.

It is easy to regard the eye in the same way: it is a body which is part of another body, whose character and constitution makes it apt for seeing with. The seeing itself is variously construed as what happens within some eyes (and beyond them in the brain) or as a mental event accompanying processes in these physical objects. If seeing is part of our conception of an eye, that is once more a matter of what we are interested in, which we must separate from our account of what exists.

Now, a separated eye is a dead eye, and separated flesh, blood and bones dead flesh, blood and bones. Is Aristotle justified in holding that they can only be called an eye, flesh, blood and bones, in an equivocal sense?

He may be justified by the consideration of the identity of the objects. This dead bone is the same bone over a period of many years by quite different criteria from those by which this living bone is the same bone over a similar period. Now as the identity is, so is the existence: that is to say, if we want to know what we say is there when we say an X is there, we shall learn by considering when we say that the same X is there. Our prejudice, then, that the existence of the eye is neutral to our interest in its function of seeing, the existence of the body neutral to our interest in the facts which mean it is a living body, is not justified.

The imagination of the living eye as existing and seeing separately is of course an absurdity. But we can perhaps imagine the eye's being taken out and preserved in separate existence as a quantity of connected living tissue. The identity of this object will then be different from the identity of a similar non-living object; for its matter changes. For Aristotle this living tissue would be the 'proximate matter' of the eye, as the bronze of which the statue consists is its proximate matter. But the reason why it is absurd to imagine the final determination which makes the eye an eye, namely its sight, as occurring in a separated eye, is that seeing is part of the life of the animal whose eye it is. This, then, will be why, consciously supposing an absurdity, Aristotle says ' if the eye could exist separately '. But when I say that seeing is part of the life of the animal, I do not mean that it is not genuinely done by the optical apparatus which we call the eye. The activity of the part, which determines it to be that part, is part of the life of the whole and except in the whole that activity does not exist, nor is the part the same, except materially. (I have deliberately left out of account the complications arising from the difference between sight as a capacity to see and as actual seeing. Aristotle says that *soul* and *the wakeful state* correspond respectively to these.) There is a contrast between the capacity to see which is sight, and the capacity to cut which an object might have without being a knife. The latter capacity can be seen in the object regardless of whether it ever cuts, but with vital capacities it is otherwise.

Aristotle is saying, then, that the soul is to the body as sight would be to the eye if the sight of the eye were not the activity just of a part, and hence a part of a life, but were itself the sum total of the life of a living thing. Souls are vegetative, when the life of the living thing consists in nutrition, growth and reproduction; animal, when to these are added sensation and locomotion; and rational, when to all these is added the activity called ' intellect ', or ' thinking of '. This alone is not the vital activity of a physical part or organ.

As we have seen, ' intellect ' is divided into two parts, the ' active ' and the passive, concept-receiving, concept-using part. This latter part Aristotle held to be perishable like the body; the former he thought was imperishable, ungenerable and eternal. Aquinas took the ' productive ' intellect to be a concept-forming part or aspect of the human mind; but from Aristotle's brief and obscure text it seems to me more likely to be the divine mind that Aristotle intends, unless, which is possible, he thought that human minds actually had a divine part: the one thing that comes into the world, as he puts it, ' from outside '.

His proof of the existence of the divine mind is as follows: First, he holds it impossible that all substances should be generable and perishable, for if they were then everything would be perishable, but change and time are perpetual; it is impossible that they should cease to be or pass away. So there are imperishable substances. These he thought to be the heavenly bodies, which he thought never to change except in place. Since, however, they do have local motion, they have potentiality and are not pure actuality in this respect, and this means that they must be moved by something else which is not in any way potential, and which therefore moves other things without itself moving or changing in any way. The only sort of thing that can set up local motion without being itself in motion is an object of desire. (It follows, of course, that what it sets in motion must be intelligences: hence the idea that the heavenly bodies are, or are carried round by, pure intelligences, which in the latter form Aquinas incorporated in his angelology.)

Why, we may ask, does Aristotle suppose that this being, which absolutely ' cannot be otherwise ' than it is, is a mind? This appears to be because of his identification of form without matter with thought. Then that which has no matter or potentiality at all is an eternal mind which always thinks. Thus there is a singular connexion between Aristotle's philosophy of logic, epistemology, and theology. There is a famous passage in the *Metaphysics* in which he has been taken at least in modern times, to say that the object of the thought of the divine mind is only its own thinking. Meinong regarded this as the most exquisitely nonsensical idea that could be conceived—the idea of thinking a thought which was of nothing but the thinking of it. I take him to have been correct; but Aristotle thought so too. The remark occurs in one of his dialectical passages, in which he raises the difficulty: ' What is the divine thought about? '—and is one of the absurdities that he derives in the course of discussing the question. For if what is thought of is thought's master, but nothing excels divine thought, must we not conclude that it is its own only object? His actual conclusion is that in some cases the thing that is understood is a science itself (presumably as opposed to material things, e.g. human bodies, being understood *by* a science), and where this is so the actuality of understanding and the actuality of its objects are one and the same. In any case a mind understands itself ' according to its participation in what it understands '; this understanding of itself is a by-product of its understanding of its object. There is thus no question of the thinking itself being the sole content of a thought, or understanding being the understanding of nothing but understanding.

The expression ' it understands itself according to its participation in what it understands ' needs some interpreting. When someone understands a thing—say, a geometrical theorem—the theorem is in him. If we want to know whether he understands that theorem, we look at what he says to see if it contains the theorem, and what we ask is: is this the theorem? It is the theorem that we ask him to expound, and not anything else which might be called the understanding of the theorem. By contrast, if he owns a piece of land or kicks a dog, he does not shew these things by shewing the land or the dog; we need further to see his title deeds, to watch or have a report on his kicking. So we may say, it is the existence of the theorem in him that is his understanding of the theorem, and not the existence of something else, namely something called understanding that goes on in relation to the theorem. This perhaps indicates what Aristotle may have meant by the identity between the actuality of the understanding and the actuality of the thing understood. As a corollary to this, we can now add that if he understands the theorem, then by that token he also understands that he understands it. For if we are satisfied that the theorem is in him, that he understands it, we shall not have a further question to settle, running: ' Do you understand *that* you understand it? Can you now give us an account, not of it, but of your understanding of it? ' His account of it is also incidentally an account of his understanding of it.

Aristotle's proof that there must be imperishable substances seems to contain more than one fallacy. He argues that if all substances were perishable, everything would be perishable; but time and change cannot begin or end but must be perpetual. Therefore there are imperishable substances. Now, in the first place, even if time and change are necessarily perpetual and without beginning, they would not be shewn not to be so by all substances being perishable, but only by its being a possibility that all substance should actually perish, in the sense that at some time there was no substance. The propositions: It is possible that all substance should perish, and: Concerning every substance, it is possible that *it* should perish, are not the same.

Secondly, it is difficult to see why Aristotle should insist that time and motion must be perpetual and without beginning. He held that time was the measure of local motion. (In this connexion we may note the singular injustice of Russell, who hated Aristotle too much to notice his work on continuity. Aristotle worked out that there could be no next moments in time and no next points in space, and Russell himself arrived at the same result; but much as he valued the result, he never gave Aristotle credit for having arrived at it.)

In view of this doctrine of Aristotle's concerning time, it seems absurd for him to hold that the non-perpetuity of time and change is impossible. It would seem that if ever there were no changeable things, there was then no change and no time. If the words ' ever ' and ' then ' sound absurd in such sentences—and this seems to be part of Aristotle's argument—the sentences can be amended so as not to contain these words. We can say e.g. that if the revolution of a certain sphere is the motion of which time is a measure, then ' at some time there were no substances ' means ' for some number n, there have been substances only during n revolutions and there have not been $n+1$ revolutions '. But to hold that there must eternally have been locally moving things because there must always have been movement because there must always have been time seems a back-to-front kind of argument.[1]

However, there is yet another argument mixed up with these, which is of more interest and is indeed the main argument. It is based on continuity: change is continuous in the same way as time; but the only change that is continuous is (circular) local motion by bodies whose movement in this way nothing can disturb; these, therefore, have no potentiality for any alteration except that they move in this way. That is to say, Aristotle takes it to be a demand of thought about the physical universe that there should be a clock made of imperishable stuff—the ' fifth substance ' (' quintessence ') which is none of the four terrestrial elements—whose motions are the universe's fundamental time-keeping process. Further, he thought that the visible heavens, with the changeless regularity of motion that they manifest, were in fact this clock. What should be said on this topic now must be dictated by the present state of scientific knowledge; it is surely a mistake to think that we have effected a separation between science and philosophy such that questions can be firmly labelled ' scientific ' or ' philosophical ' and discussed by different parties, each ignorant of the other's discipline.

Aristotle speaks with respect of the popular ancient traditions

[1] I do not myself wish to argue *in propria persona* that time need not be perpetual—for I doubt the sense of asking ' Has time always been or did it begin? ' But if it is reasonable to speak in this way at all, then I should want to argue with Aristotle as above.

concerning the divinity of the heavenly bodies (though with contempt of the mythological accretions to this central idea). This was
no doubt because he conceived the various heavenly spheres involved
in his astronomy, to have intellect. We have seen why they had to
have intellect: they were the *prima mobilia*, which are moved by an
unmoving mover, and so by an object of desire; they therefore have
intellect. But intellect itself, or mind, is clearly for him the same
thing as God. The divine intellect itself, the unmoved mover, is
mind without any ' accidents ' at all; i.e., no predicates hold of it (a)
which indicate something existing *in* it, and (b) whose combination
with the subject therefore yields a description of a *per accidens*
existent, according to the logical doctrine that I described earlier.
Other things that have intellect are also the subjects of *per accidens*
predications; but Aristotle seems to have felt that the intellect which
was part of their substantial existence was as it were a bit of divinity
in them. For him ' mind and God ' is a hendiadys; he says for
example in the *Ethics* that ' good in the category of substance is
mind and God, as in the category of time it is the opportune '. That
is to say, as ' opportune '=' at a good time ', so ' mind and God '=
' good substance '.

There is of course a very great deal in Aristotle that I have not
considered. The foregoing account of certain of his central themes
may at least have made it clear—unfortunate as this is—how inaccessible he is to all who are not willing to study the actual Greek texts with
the aid of both scholarship and philosophical acumen. I wish that I
had more of both, and can hope only to have suggested both how
rich a field Aristotle's writings could prove to philosophers of the
present day ' analytic ' schools, and how relevant philosophical
investigation into the subject matters themselves is to the work of
Aristotelian scholars. Inability to philosophise would render a
scholar incompetent to grasp Aristotle's ideas, of which he would be
likely to give a philosophically too easy, as well as a merely external,
account; moreover, not every style of philosophising will help him
here, but in some ways some current methods will be of use; on the
other hand, modern philosophers, without scholarship, will be able
to make little of Aristotle's more difficult writings that is relevant to
what he actually thought or to genuine philosophic enquiry. But a
philosopher of the modern schools, who is no longer under the influence of certain assumptions which have been common since Descartes

and Locke, should find a great deal to stimulate him and a great deal from which he can learn, in these writings. Our present situation is unique in philosophical history: our period is one of intense philosophical activity, and also we are now in a position to read Aristotle critically and at the same time with sympathy—without either servility or hostility. We can find it very profitable to do so, so long as we avoid what is perhaps an especial danger: that of being patronising. We can avoid this if we realise that many of the questions that are central in him have by no means been settled. For example, the questions discussed here, belonging to the philosophy of logic and to the theory of meaning, are wide open, and Aristotle's contribution to the discussion of these, whether right or wrong, is unique and is not naif.

AQUINAS

Thomas of Aquino (*Aquinas*), a cadet of a noble Italian family, was born in the Castle of Rocca Secca in 1225. Like Talleyrand, he was destined by his parents for an ecclesiastical career because of a lame leg; but his family's hopes of his becoming a Benedictine monk, and ultimately Abbot of Monte Cassino, were spoiled by his decision to seek his vocation in the new Dominican order of begging friars. This led to violent opposition from his family; they kidnapped him while travelling with other Dominicans and imprisoned him in a tower of the castle, where he spent his time learning the Bible by heart. Eventually he escaped in a basket lowered from the castle window by his sisters, and after an appeal to the Pope was allowed to follow his vocation.

He studied philosophy and theology at Paris under St. Albert the Great, who early appreciated his genius. After taking his Bachelor's degree (1248) he accompanied St. Albert to Cologne, where he taught for four years before returning to Paris to prepare for his Doctorate, which he received at an unusually early age in 1256. In the mean time, along with St. Bonaventure as representative of the Franciscans, he had successfully defended the cause of the friars before the Pope.

In his lifetime as a Dominican, Aquinas laboured incessantly in teaching, preaching, and writing; at the same time, he was most scrupulous in observing his religious duties of saying Mass and singing the Divine Office in the choir of his priory, and spent many hours in prayer. When the Feast of Corpus Christi was instituted for the whole Church, Aquinas was chosen to write the

Office of the Feast, and on this occasion wrote his famous Eucharistic hymns.

The last years of Aquinas's life were spent in writing his masterpiece the ' Summa Theologica '. This was left unfinished; a few months before his death, while saying Mass, he was granted a vision in comparison with which all his theological labours appeared ' as straw ', and he had not the heart to write again. He was already ailing when summoned to attend the Council of Lyons, and died upon the journey (March 7th, 1274). He was canonized in 1323.

Aquinas was a large, heavy man, slow to speak, and habitually absent-minded; he was loved in his community for his unfailing courtesy, helpfulness, and good temper. The miraculous legends that have gathered around his name give a distinct impression of his personality. One relates that on being visited by the apparition of his sister from Purgatory, he asked her a question about the mode of knowledge employed by souls separated from the body. Another relates his visit to a holy nun who used to be levitated in ecstasy; Aquinas remarked that her feet were very large; this made her come out of her ecstasy in indignation at his rudeness, whereupon he gently advised her to seek greater humility.

AQUINAS, like Aristotle, ranges over a vast variety of subjects: an account of his thought must therefore be either an unilluminating sketch or a very selective commentary. I have attempted the latter: the first part of this essay discusses some of Aquinas's fundamental terms, the second outlines his teaching in natural theology.

I

(1) *Matter*. Under this heading I shall discuss only the primary meaning of Aquinas's term ' *materia* '—what he also called *materia prima*. This term pretty well corresponds in its use to some uses of the word ' stuff ' in English. Boys who are starting chemistry are often shown an experiment in which the stuff in a vessel undergoes some striking change: there is the same *stuff* in the vessel before and after the change, but there is not the same chemical substance. Now it is in this sort of case that Aquinas would have spoken of the same *matter* assuming now one form and now another. Or again, when the stuff that Miss T. eats turns into Miss T., Aquinas would say that the same matter was first (say) bread and then part of a human body.

The elementary chemical experiment I mentioned would often be used to establish the ' conservation of mass ', the vessel being weighed, with an identical result, before and after the experiment: it would of course be an anachronism to use any such idea in expounding Aquinas, and we must equally beware of supposing that ' conservation of mass ' is part of what we now *mean* by there being the same stuff in a vessel. It is a matter of common observation that though vessels leak, some leak less than others; the ideal of an unleaky vessel is as easily conceived as that of a rigid body, and it was known, long before there was any idea of ' conservation of mass ', that a hermetically sealed vessel is almost ideally unleaky. ' Conservation of mass ' is now known to be a good *test* for a vessel's ' being unleaky ', or ' containing the same stuff '; but it is not what we *mean* by these expressions. And even when mass is conserved, the question of there being the same stuff may be open: one may e.g. ask whether a glass of water that stands on a scalepan is the same stuff all the time or is undergoing some interchange of stuff with the air, even if we need

G

not adjust the weights in the other scale. Now it is no anachronism to tie up this sort of question with what Aquinas meant by matter: we find in him, for example, an elaborate discussion of what is now called metabolism—that is, the interchange of matter between an organism and its environment—and he comes to the conclusion that the continued identity of an animal does not involve that its body retains *any* of the same matter *all* the time.

The question may naturally be raised: If the matter or stuff is e.g. first wine and then vinegar, what then is it throughout the process? And the early Greek philosophers—Aquinas's *antiqui naturales*— tried to answer this question by using the name of some familiar substance like air or water. In our time the psychologically satis- factory answer (given by popularizers of science) would be that electricity appears now under the form of one substance, now under that of another—electricity being undertood as the mysterious but familiar stuff that runs along wires and gives you shocks.

Following Aristotle, Aquinas held that it was a mistake to try to find any such answer. The same matter was wine and is vinegar; when it was wine, it was wine and nothing else, and now it is vinegar and nothing else; there is no kind of substance—water or air or electricity—that it is all the time. Likewise, there is no quality (like colour or temperature), or size, or other attribute, that the same matter has to have all the time. All that we can say holds of the same matter all the time is that it has the capacity or potentiality of being one or other kind of substance (within a certain range), and of having qualities within certain ranges, size within a certain range, etc. Within these ranges of potentialities, now one, now another will be actualized; but there is not any that has to be actualized all the time.

There are, of course, general difficulties about the notion of potentiality; but if for the moment we take that notion for granted, there is no added difficulty about Aquinas's notion of matter. It is important not to confuse ' the matter of a body is not actually any- thing all the time ' (i.e. ' there is nothing it actually is all the time ') with ' the matter of a body is all the time not actually anything, i.e. it is a permanently bare potentiality '. Even if some unguarded expressions used by Aquinas would apparently support the latter assertion, it is contrary to his explicit doctrine. For example, he several times states that, in virtue of whichever form it has at the moment, the matter is made to be an actual thing (*fit ens actu*); and matter apart from form is a contradiction in terms, unrealizable even by Divine power; so a given parcel of matter always has some actual attributes—only not always the same ones.

Again, Aquinas discusses a difference between such statements as ' white has the potentiality of being black and ' gas (*aer*) has the potentiality of being flame '. In the first, the subject-term ' white ' refers to a body that is white, and that same body has the potentiality of being black; *white* is not a constituent (*pars*) of the body in question. In the second statement, we are really using the figure of speech called *synecdoche*, in which we predicate of a whole what is properly predicable of its part (as when we say that a man brought home a bottle of wine and drank it, when he really drank only the wine, not the bottle); for it is not really the gas, Aquinas would say, that has the potentiality of being flame—when the flame comes to be, the gas will have ceased to be. What has the potentiality of being flame is a constituent (*pars*) of the gas—something in the gas that now has the form of gas but could have the form of flame—and (though in the passage I am citing the word is not used) Aquinas is clearly referring to the *matter* of the gas: the same matter as is now gas can be flame, and the gas will cease to exist when the matter that is now gas is gas no longer. (IIIa 9. 75 art. 8.)

People often put forward as Aquinas's a more ' subtle ' account of matter than this; they are suffering, it appears to me, from the confusion just mentioned, between ' is not actually anything all the time ' and ' is all the time not actually anything ', and so regard themselves (and Aquinas) as committed to defending the notion of a permanently bare potentiality. It is to be feared that, because Aquinas rightly says matter is not intelligible on its own account (sc. but only as a constituent of bodies, in which it occurs under some form or other), they regard an unintelligible account of matter as being on the face of it the more acceptable one. Further, they are confused as to the relation between the statements (say): ' this matter is now gas '; ' this matter now has the form of gas '; ' this matter is now the subject of the form of gas '. If the second and third of these are to be defensible at all, they must be philosophical re-phrasings of the first, as ' John stands in the relation *wiser than* to James ' is of ' John is wiser than James '; but there are people prepared to say that just because the matter *is the subject of* successive forms, it never *has* any form at all.

It is a serious question how Aquinas's conception of matter

squares with our modern scientific knowledge. To say there is *no* room for the conception of *the same matter* or *the same stuff* in modern science would indeed be wrong; a scientist might very well investigate whether, and how fast, an apparently unchanging body was in fact undergoing an interchange of matter with the environment; or again he might want to know which parts of a man's body were nourished by a given substance, and perhaps use radioactive 'tracers' to show where the ingested stuff went. But the application of such talk to fundamental physics seems out of the question; the identification of parcels of matter seems here to lose its sense, and so indeed does the ideal of a perfectly unleaky vessel.

It would take us too far to go into these difficulties further; but at any rate it is no way out of the difficulty to cut adrift the notion of matter from the connexions it has in Aquinas with what we now call chemical changes and with the metabolism of living things, and to make it a more 'philosophical' notion. As I have said, the more 'philosophical' notion that is aimed at appears to me mere nonsense; what I take to have been Aquinas's notion is not nonsense, but it is arguable that the progress of science has rendered it unusable in a fundamental account of the physical world. If this should turn out to be the position, it is better to say so outright than to preserve a verbal loyalty to Aquinas by using his terms while evacuating them of the meaning they bore for him.

We must now consider the sense in which matter is 'the principle of individuation'. This last phrase often serves to cover up a conflation of two quite different problems: (i) What constitutes the identity of one individual of a kind (e.g. there being one and the same cat) over a period of time? (ii) What constitutes the difference between two individuals of the same kind (e.g. two pennies) at a given time? It ought to be clear off hand that these are different problems: for we cannot argue e.g. that an old man is not the same human being as a baby seventy years earlier, because a coexisting baby and old man would be different human beings.

In Aquinas the problems are kept clearly apart. For him, the identity of a given thing of a kind over a period of time does not involve any persistence of the same matter throughout: a flame, or a living thing, is all the time undergoing an interchange of matter with its environment, an interchange which in the end may be total— as Sir John Cutler's silk stockings, often mended with worsted, had in the end no silk in them. (This case again serves to distinguish the two problems of ' the principle of individuation '; it is nothing against the stockings ' being the same pair from first to last, that *coexisting* silk and worsted stockings would be different pairs.)

On the other hand, two individuals of the same kind that coexist are, for Aquinas, distinguished by differences of matter. Two pennies that coexist may in fact differ in all sorts of respects—one may be in mint condition and the other bent, defaced and stained—but these cannot be what make the pennies two: if there were not in any case two pennies, they could not acquire these differenes. What makes the two pennies to be two is that they are two pieces of matter; if this assertion appears trivial, it is because the vocabulary used by Aquinas has passed so much into common speech. And that it is the same notion of matter we are using here as we were using about the generation and corruption of substances may be shown thus: The sense of ' matter ' in which we say that the two pennies are different pieces of matter is the same sense as that in which we say that the same matter changes from being in one piece to being in several pieces, or vice versa; and this in turn is clearly the same sense of ' the same matter' as that in which we say that the same matter is now gas, now flame, or now wine, now vinegar.

This brings us to Aquinas's theory of quantity, continuous and discrete, and its connexion with individuation. Discrete quantity or ' number ' (*numerus*) is that attribute whose different species are expressed by the predicates ' being in one piece ', ' being in n pieces '; it is one of the attributes in respect of which the same matter can undergo change. It appears to me that Aquinas was right both in recognising this attribute of things, and in refusing to hold that numerical terms *always* refer to this attribute of things (as some of his contemporaries seem to have held).

Aquinas rightly remarked that numerical terms can be applied wherever things can be identified and distinguished at all; thus, we can speak of the nineteen figures of syllogism, or the three Divine Persons; and this is not a far-fetched metaphor from spatial divisions. Number, in the sense in which it does *not* mean: being in so many pieces, is what Aquinas calls transcendental; this does not mean something grand and mysterious, but merely what is now meant by ' topic-neutral ' as Professor Ryle uses it; you would know *nothing* as to the topic of a conversation if you merely heard number-words occurring in it from time to time. In spite of this, Aquinas accepts Aristotle's teaching that mathematics essentially deals with spatial reality. On his own showing, this is clearly wrong; an addition-sum may be applied to the results of counting any sort of objects, and Aquinas rightly holds that countable objects may be non-spatial.

As regards extension, or continuous quantity, Aquinas draws attention to an important feature in which this differs from other attributes. I shall introduce this feature in a slightly different way from Aquinas. If two things are both red and the same shade of red, this tells us everything about their colour-relationship; but if each of two things has just the same geometrical attributes—the same size and shape—this does not tell us everything about their geometrical relationship. Two equal circles may form very various geometrical configurations according to their relative position. To put this another way, closer to Aquinas: Two instances e.g. of the same colour differ only in that there are (otherwise) different things that are coloured; but two instances of the same geometrical attributes—e.g. two circles of equal size—may differ in a strictly geometrical way (viz in relative position), without our having to appeal to the *circular things*' being *already* different.

Aristotle had tried to explain the difference between two *circles*, as opposed to that between two *circular things* like pennies, by saying that it was a difference in ' intelligible ' matter, whereas the difference between two pennies is a difference in ' sensible ' matter; and there are passages (made much of by neo-scholastics) in which Aquinas repeats these dark sayings of the Philosopher. Aquinas's originality comes out when in other passages he states something quite different: that geometrical attributes are self-individuating; do not owe their individuation to being attributes of different things, or to inhering in different matter (of any brand), but just *are* individuated, in their own right. (See e.g. IIIa q. 77 art. 2.)

It is this individuation of geometrical attributes that accounts for the individuation of coexisting pieces of matter; and so Aquinas's final account of the ' principle of individuation ' in this sense is that it is matter marked out (*signata*) by dimensive quality. Similarly, we need dimensive quantity to account for the individuation of different parts in a single substance. As we shall see, the body of an animal is for Aquinas a single substance, so its parts cannot be distinguished in terms of attributes' belonging to different things; rather, one eye, say, is differentiated from the other because their matter is geometrically differentiated.

(2) *Form*. According to the ' philosophical ' view of matter, which, I have argued, was not Aquinas's, we come to know matter by mentally stripping off the forms which clothe it—a procedure that requires a high development of the abstractive power. Now obviously this procedure could not begin unless we clearly knew what was this *form* that was to be stripped off; the conception of matter would thus be an advanced development from that of form. This is historically quite wrong: as Aristotle pointed out, the early Greek philosophers attained (even though imperfectly) to some conception of a matter determinable to various kinds of substance before they had any general notion of form. ' Matter,' he said, ' is in a way easy; form is frightfully puzzling '. And the reason why he found form frightfully puzzling was that he did not reach the conception of matter by a stripping away of forms from the concrete substance, but contrariwise reached the conception of form as that which is added to a parcel of matter to make a concrete substance. Form is the concrete substance *minus* its matter; it is *this* subtraction that is difficult; and I do not think Aristotle ever really mastered the technique of this dissection— there is hardly a statement about form in the *Metaphysics* that is not (at least verbally) contradicted by some other statement. On matter Aquinas was largely content to expound Aristotle; but he had to work strenuously to overcome the difficulties about form, and here he had to explore territory that Aristotle had only skirted.

To this view that it is form rather than matter which is difficult to understand it may be objected that both Aristotle and Aquinas constantly treat the formal element in material things as what makes them intelligible. This objection, however, would involve a muddle. To understand the nature e.g. of a cat is to understand how a parcel of matter is organized into a cat, and this organization (for Aristotle and Aquinas) constitutes the form; thus that which in fact constitutes the form of a thing is that which is intelligible in the thing. Matter is intelligible only as a capacity for this or that form—i.e. for being this or that kind of substance; and concerning capacity in general it holds good that it can be understood, or even described, only in terms of what it is a capacity for. But it does not follow, because that which in fact constitutes a form is intelligible, that the *notion* of form must be transparently intelligible and not ' frightfully puzzling '; and

the question obviously is frightfully puzzling, how that which constitutes a parcel of matter as a cat is related to the cat so constituted.

Let us consider how these puzzles would have presented themselves to Aristotle. ' If I say ' Bucephalus is a horse ', then I am
saying concerning Bucephalus what he *is*, not what he is related to;
I am not saying that Bucephalus imitates or partakes of The Horse, as
Platonists have thought; what Bucephalus is is a horse, not a form.
And yet it is the predicate ' a horse ' that tells me what makes that
parcel of matter to be what it is; so this predicate must mean the
form after all. But again, ' horse ' must mean matter, as well as
form, because in any horse there is matter; yet it must not mean any
particular matter. Again, is the form different in different horses; or
is it the same, and only the matter different? Again, are there many
forms in one individual, and if so how are they related? '

One step Aquinas took towards the solution was to formulate a
logical theory of predication. On his view, a general term like ' horse '
signifies in a radically different way when it stands as a logical subject
e.g. in ' a horse is in the tulip bed ' and when it stands as a logical
predicate in ' Bucephalus is a horse '; such a general term in subject
position refers to a concrete thing (*suppositum*), whereas in predicate
position it refers to a form or a nature (essence). (This last ' or '
expresses an alternative, not a licence to choose between synonyms;
the difference between ' form ' and ' nature ' or ' essence ' will be
discussed later. For simplicity's sake I shall for the moment speak of
form, and of nature or essence, without discrimination; a ' nature '
referred to by a predicate will in any event *include* a form.) Thus
Aquinas affirms that ' a horse ' in ' Bucephalus is a horse ' signifies a
nature, but denies that Bucephalus is being asserted to *be* (identical
with) that nature.

Aristotle was impeded from such a clear-cut solution in two ways.
First, there is no linguistic (inflexional) distinction between subject
and predicate uses of a term in Greek; this is a mere accidental
feature of language, even though it is true of many other languages;
for there is an inflexional distinction in Polish, and a Pole would e.g.
instinctively use the predicative (instrumental) form for ' King ' and
the nominative form for ' Louis XIV ' in ' the then King of France
was Louis XIV ', where users of other languages would have no
feeling for which was subject and which predicate. More important
was Aristotle's fear of Platonistic mythology: if Bucephalus is not

identical with the nature signified by ' a horse ' he will surely be somehow *related* to it, and then shall we not get back to a Platonic Idea and all the difficulties of imitation or participation?

Ockham and others sought to cut the Gordian knot by a two-name theory of predication: that ' Bucephalus is a horse ' is true because ' Bucephalus ' stands for one of the things that ' a horse ' also stands for. Ockham jeers at ' certain ignorant people ' (meaning Aquinas) who say that a general term standing as a predicate refers to a form; for then in ' Socrates is white ' ' white ' would mean the form whiteness, but ' Whiteness is white ' is false. But this simple theory runs into horrid complications when Ockham tries to carry it through— just as, if you insist on explaining planetary motions in terms of simple uniform revolutions, you will need a great number of revolutions.

It will be enough to mention one striking puzzle of Ockham's own. It is clear that ' a philosopher ' occurs in the same predicative way in ' Socrates became a philosopher ' as in ' Socrates was a philosopher '. But if, as Ockham thinks, ' a philosopher ' stands for a philosopher, which philosopher then did Socrates become? Socrates did not become Socrates; nor did he become any other philosopher. Ockham to be sure finds a way out: if we expound our puzzling proposition as ' first of all Socrates was not a philosopher, and later on Socrates was a philosopher ', we may say that in the ' first of all ' clause ' a philosopher ' refers distributively to each philosopher that Socrates then was not; whereas the question which philosopher Socrates was later on—admits of the answer ' Socrates '! But it ought to be clear that this is a cul-de-sac.

To get a clear view of Aquinas's way out, let us consider phrases of the type ' the wisdom of Socrates '. The same sort of puzzle as arises over the relation that it seems ' is ' in ' Socrates is wise ' must signify if it does not signify that Socrates *is identically* one of the wise, arises also over the ' of ' (or Latin genitive inflexion) in ' the wisdom of Socrates '. Philosophers try to construe this as ' wisdom that belongs to Socrates '; and then they ask what sort of entity wisdom is, and what sort of relation is here signified by ' belongs to '.

These discussions are, as Wittgenstein put it, like barbarian misconstructions of civilized man's language. It is as though someone asked in regard to ' the square root of 4 ' what ' the ' square root was, or how one number can be ' of ', belong to, another number. Logically, we must divide the phrase thus: ' the square root of/4 '; the first part of the phrase (or, better, the circumstance that this is followed by some number-expression or other) is the sign of a *function*, and the ' of ' (or the genitive inflexion in other languages) does not stand for a special relation of *belonging to*, but indicates the way that the sign for a function needs completion with the sign of an *argument*. (This matter is fully gone into in the chapter on Frege in the present work.)

Similarly, we must divide ' the wisdom of/Socrates ' in the way shown: the first part of the phrase (or, better, the circumstance that it is followed by the name of an individual thing) is the sign of a *form;* the ' of ', or the genitive inflexion, does not signify special relation, but merely indicates how the sign of a form needs completion with the sign of an object whose form it is. ' Wisdom ' *tout court* means nothing in heaven or earth; wisdom is always wisdom-of —as Aquinas puts it, it is of-something (*entis*) rather than itself something (*ens*). A Platonist's belief in Wisdom is like my barbarian's wonder what The Square Root might be.

We may now go back to the predication ' Socrates is wise '. For Aquinas, the same form is signified by the predicate ' — is wise ' and by ' the wisdom of— ', which call for the same sort of completion; only the manner of referring to the form (*modus significandi*) is different. In ' Socrates is wise ' we are using an expression for a form to frame the supposition that that form is a form of a given individual; we use ' the wisdom of Socrates ' when we want to talk *about* this form—to make *it* the subject-matter of our discourse.

Aquinas insists that what can be said of forms cannot significantly, let alone truly, be said of individuals; only in connexion with a general term, signifying a form or nature, can we ask the question ' one or many? '; it is (not just false, but) sheerly unintelligible to speak of the plurality of a named individual. If I say there are many suns, ' suns ' is not the plural of the proper name ' Sun ' but of a descriptive term—whether in fact that term applies to one or to many things, its plural is intelligible if and only if it is a general descriptive term (*nomen naturae*). In *De Ente et Essentia* Aquinas clearly explains that it makes no difference to what it is for a thing to be (say) a man, how many men there may be: unity or plurality is incidental (*accidit*) to the form or nature that has one or more instances.

When we see that the answer to the question ' one or many ?' is an assertion about a form or nature, we can see also the radical mistakenness of the Platonic doctrine that the form signified by a general term is ' one over against many '; on the contrary, when I ask ' are there many ——s or only one? ' the general term I use in the plural stands for a form or nature, and there being one *or* there being many may alike attach to that form or nature. To be sure, if the question is put in the shape ' has the form or nature: *being* ——: got many instances or only one? ', the illusion of ' one over against many ' reappears. But such a grammatically singular expression as ' the form or nature: *being a man* ' must not, on Aquinas's view, be taken as anything more than a dispensable manner of speaking; if we look for a single thing named by it, we fall into nonsense.

Aquinas is thus firmly and thoroughly anti-Platonic about forms. Faced with the authority of the Platonizing pseudo-Dionysius, who believed in a whole hierarchy of hypostatized abstractions like Life and Intellect, culminating in the One, of which we can only say ' One is One and all alone and ever more shall be so '—Aquinas blandly denies that the (supposed) disciple of St. Paul could possibly have meant what he said. It appears quite wrong to suppose that because Aquinas accepted the authenticity of pseudo-Dionysius, he was specially influenced by his doctrine.

The expression for a form is either a logical predicate like ' — is red ', or, in subject-position, an expression requiring completion with the name of an individual—' the redness of— ', or equivalently ' that by which ' (sc. ' in virtue of which ')'—is red '. The last two types of expression (the second of them specially common in Aquinas) are reminiscent of functional signs in mathematics like ' log ' or ' sin ', which are completable by numerical signs. Now in the mathematical case, when we supply a numerical sign of what is called an ' argument' along with a functional sign, we get an expression signifying the value of the function for that argument, e.g. ' log 2 ' or ' sin 2 '. What sort of entity, then, is signified by expressions of the type ' the redness of A' or ' that by which A is red '?

At this point we must notice a certain verbal confusion in Aquinas —I believe only verbal. He uses the same word ' form ' *both* for what is symbolized by ' the wisdom of . . . ' (or by the fact that this expression is followed by the name of an individual) *and* for what is symbolized by a phrase completed with the name of an individual, like ' the wisdom of *Socrates* '. The syntax of the Latin language, in which 'of Socrates' is rendered by an inflexion of the word 'Socrates', could not but obscure the matter: the real sign for the form would be something not readily picked out by eye, as ' the wisdom of . . . ' is in English, since it consists of the noun ' *sapientia* ' plus the genitive inflexion of the following noun.

Moreover, our mathematical analogy of functions was not available to Aquinas; and it is not free from dangers of its own, for people often fall into a confusion about functions just like the confusion about forms that I am trying to avoid. For example: one variable quantity, say the length of a rod, may be a function *of* another variable quantity, say temperature; but if we write this in mathematical form, $l = f(T)$, the function is represented not by ' f (T) ' but by ' f ( ) ', and we must not say that the function *is* a variable quantity or a quantity at all; nor must we say that the length is a function *tout court*, only that it is a function *of* the temperature. (The verbal difficulties that inescapably arise here are fully discussed in the chapter on Frege.)

To avoid these dangers of ambiguity, with the least departure from Aquinas's own style of language and thought, I propose to speak of entities symbolized by predicates or by expressions like ' the wisdom of . . . ' as *forms, tout court;* of those symbolized by expressions like ' the wisdom of Socrates ', as *individualized forms.* An individualized form will then be a form *of* or *in* an individual, but will not be a form *tout court:* just as 4 is a function *of* 2, namely its double or its square, but is not a function *tout court.* A form is as it were a function that takes an individualized form as its value for a given individual as argument.

Aquinas does explicitly speak of a form as being multipliable in itself, but individualized by occurring in a subject; but I do not know of any place where he explicitly says that a form once individualized by occurring in a subject is no longer a form *tout court* (a form *simpliciter,* as he would say). There are however many passages where he clearly means a phrase like ' the wisdom of Socrates ' to refer to something no less individual, no more multipliable, than Socrates himself is; so even though he does apply the word ' form ' *tout court* to this sort of entity, we must either take this use of ' form ' to convey a different sense from that in which forms are said to be multipliable, or else regard Aquinas's theory of form as merely chaotic and incoherent. My own view is that Aquinas is mostly guilty only of a verbal obscurity that is easily removed by always referring to *individualized* forms by their full title where there is any risk of ambiguity; the correctness of this view is to be established not by particular proof-texts, but by its facilitating a coherent synoptic account of Aquinas's thought.

Aquinas's notion of an individualized form corresponds to an important use of the verb ' to make ' or ' *facere* ': as when we say that what ' makes ' a lump of brass spherical is its surface. Now here ' that by which ' (*quo*) the lump is spherical is easily regarded as an individual thing with attributes (e.g. colour), no less than ' that which ' (*quod*) is spherical. It is not surprising that the case should be specially clear: form is actually named from this specially clear case—shape. And as regards dimensive quantity, again, we have already considered Aquinas's reason for speaking of its individuation; the extension of a body is in a sense individual in its own right, and is not to be identified with the body whose extension it is.

In a case like colour, we may be more inclined to think of that which ' makes ' a thing red as being a universal *in rebus*, and the existence of an *individualized* form is far from obvious. But even here an anti-Platonic argument is not hard to construct. Redness is not colour (colouredness) plus a distinguishable *differentia*; that which is added to colour to constitute redness can only be redness over again; and in a red pane of glass there are not two features, one making it barely coloured, the other making it red. Yet if in this pane it is one and the same feature that makes it coloured and makes it red, then by parity of reasoning in that pane it is one and the same feature that makes it coloured and makes it green. How can being coloured be the same feature as being red *and* the same feature as being green?

This puzzle can be cleared up in terms of individualized forms. That which ' makes ' A to be coloured is the very same individualized form as that which ' makes ' A to be red; that which ' makes ' B to be coloured is the very same individualized form as that which ' makes ' B to be green; on the other hand, ' the colour of — ', ' the redness of — ', ' the greenness of — ', all differ in significance—there are, so to say, three different functions, of which the first and the second have the same value for A as argument and the first and the third have the same value for B as argument; just as the square of x is the double of x if x is 2 and the treble of x if x is 3.

Another important application of this line of thought is to *good-ness*. In the sense of ' makes ' in which what makes a table brown is its colour or its brownness, it is impossible that the *only* answer to the question ' What makes so-and-so good? ' should be ' Its goodness ' or ' Its intrinsic worth '; there must always be some attributes other than goodness whose possession makes the thing good. Now the relation between goodness and the attribute that makes a thing good has been an intractable puzzle to modern philosophers. Broadly speaking, they have had three types of theory: (i) an identification of goodness, by definition, with some particular good-making attribute (theories of this sort are said by their opponents to exemplify the ' naturalistic fallacy '); (ii) a view that the adjective ' good ' in its primary acceptation has commendatory or prescriptive, not descriptive, force; (iii) a view that goodness is an odd ' non-natural ' attribute, united by a queer (non-logical and non-causal) ' must ' to the good-making characteristics.

In my opinion all three turn out to be blind alleys; in any case, it is worth noticing that Aquinas offers a fourth alternative. Goodness as such is not identifiable with any special good-making characteristic: but for any given good thing there is a good-making characteristic whose possession by the thing is precisely what ' makes ' that thing good, in the sense of ' make ' that we have been considering. Here again our analogy of functions works. There is no multiple of a number that is *always* the square of the number; but for any given number you can find a multiple of it that is its square—the double for 2, the quadruple for 4, and so on. Similarly, there is no *one* good-making characteristic whose inclusion in the description of a thing ensures the thing's goodness; but for any given good thing you can find a good-making characteristic X such that *for that thing* to be good is the same as *for that thing* to be X (the thing is good and is X in virtue of the same individualized form); so that ' good ' adds being X to the description of this thing, and is not void of descriptive force.

Perhaps the most important case of identity for individualized forms is that of *substantial* forms. A piece of matter cannot be an actual thing except in virtue of some form; Aquinas insists that there can be only *one* (individualized) form that so constitutes a piece of matter as an actual thing—other (individualized) forms are logically posterior to its being an actual thing, and ' make ' it not to be an actual thing but to be such-and-such a thing, e.g. to be brown or square. On the other hand, it will for Aquinas be one and the same individualized form that makes my cat Tibbles to be an actual thing, a single bodily substance; to be a living thing; to be an animal; and to be a cat. This is called a *substantial* form, in contrast with Tibbles's colour, weight, size, posture, etc., which are *accidents* or *accidental* forms.

The individualized substantial form of a living thing if called a *soul* (*anima*); but the term must not be given an animistic meaning. The continued existence of Tibbles consists in there being this individualized life in a continuously changing parcel of matter; when the parcel of matter that at some moment goes to make up Tibbles ceases to be a living organism at all, the 'soul' of Tibbles does not depart to a Happy Hunting Ground but just ceases to be; and the matter ceases to be a single bodily thing, as it was in virtue of that individualized form, and becomes a mere jumble of substances. (How Aquinas could think things were otherwise for human beings will be discussed later on.)

At this point Aristotle would insist that it is not just a soul or form that makes Tibbles to be an animal, for it belongs to the definition of 'animal' that there should be form *in matter*. Thus it looks as though that which makes Tibbles to be an animal (or a cat, or for that matter a single bodily substance) were not just an individualized form, a 'soul' in the sense just explained, but 'soul' plus matter; Aquinas accepts this result. As regards this 'soul'-plus-matter, there was a chronic medieval perplexity: Is this 'nature' or 'essence' of Tibbles really or only conceptually distinct from Tibbles himself? Aquinas holds there is a real distinction; one proof of this is afforded by the fact of metabolism. Tibbles himself consists at a given moment, of a 'soul' existing in a given parcel of matter; but his 'essence' or 'nature' consists of that 'soul' plus *matter*, not: plus a given parcel of matter; for Tibbles remains a cat, and the same cat, in spite of a thoroughgoing metabolism, and his 'essence' is precisely that in virtue of which this continues to hold true of him. Or again: flesh and bones belong to the 'essence' of Tibbles, but—as the facts of metabolism require—not *this* flesh and *this* bone, the actual bits of flesh and bone that are now in Tibbles; so there is something in Tibbles that is not in his 'essence'.

We may well think, however, that Aquinas's 'essence' is a

chimerical entity. How can there be flesh and bones that are not *this* flesh and *these* bones? or matter that is not *this* matter? ' Essence ' looks to be as absurd a construction as Meinong's indefinite man. To be sure, one sort of expression that Aquinas takes to refer to the ' essence ' or ' nature ' of a thing—' Socrates in so far as he is a man ' —both has an unquestionably legitimate use as a *grammatical* subject of predicates, and has an appearance of being a singular referring expression; but may not the appearance be misleading?

To answer this objection, we must first notice that for Aquinas ' this matter ' is not related to ' matter ' as ' this red ' is to ' red '; ' matter ' is not a general term applicable to particular pieces of matter. This matter is matter individuated in *this* way; and for Aquinas the same matter may now be individuated in this way and now not individuated at all; thus, if two glasses of water are poured together into a jug, the same matter was in the two glasses and is now in the jug, but he would hold that no part of the water in the jug is identifiable as that which was in one of the glasses. (In view of this, it is not at all clear that a breakdown of identifiability at the microscopic level is fatal to Aquinas's conception of matter.)

Accordingly, when we consider *this* matter, matter identifiable in *this* way, there is for Aquinas a real, not just a conceptual, distinction between the matter and the way it is currently individuated: and it is this real distinction that makes it possible to say that the essence of Tibbles or Socrates contains matter, but not *this* matter. And if it is possible to say this, it is possible also to say that the essence contains flesh and bones, but not *this* flesh or *these* bones. For ' *this* flesh ' here means ' *this* matter, possessed of the attributes of flesh '; and if *this* matter is no part of the essence of Tibbles, neither is *this* flesh; for, owing to metabolism, neither *this* matter nor (any speci- fiable part of) *this* flesh remains permanently in Tibbles. But if matter exists under Tibbles's individualized cat-form, this requires that some of the matter shall possess the attributes of flesh and bones; and this is how flesh and bone belong to Tibbles's essence—not because there exist indefinite flesh and indefinite bones.

Though the essences of this cat and that cat are not identical— they contain different individualized forms—they are exactly alike, and so a single mental likeness (*species*) in a man's mind can corres- pond to both. Here we must notice a class of statements in which a general term like ' man ' is used as a subject of predication to refer to the nature or essence: a true example of this class would be ' man is an animal ', false ones would be ' man is a spirit ' or ' man is a machine '. Such statements are not quantifiable—it is not in question whether every man or some man is meant; the predicate is (allegedly) one that holds *in virtue of* the human nature signified by the subject. Plato would have taken such statements to be true or false statements about the Form Man, which is ' one over against the many '; but Aquinas in his *De Ente et Essentia* shows why this view cannot be correct. A predicate that is truly attachable to the subject ' man ', used in the manner we are considering, holds good of any individual man; but such predicates as ' is a Form ', ' is one over against many ', etc., certainly do not so hold good of individual men. The possibility of true statements like ' man is an animal ' does not depend on a real unity of human nature in all men, but on there not being relevant differences between the human nature of this man and that man.

Aquinas held that our use of general terms for the natures of material things marks the point at which our mind grasps reality most directly and most firmly. Such terms answer the question ' *quid est?* ', which has in common Latin usage a much more restricted meaning than the corresponding question ' what is it? ' has in English: hence the use of the barbarous abstract noun ' quiddity ' as a synonym for ' nature ' and ' essence '. It may well be thought that Aquinas exaggerated the extent to which we do get at the quiddities of things: on reading, e.g. that the word ' stone ' expresses our definition of stone, whereby we know what stone is, a geologist may well wonder what Aquinas would have offered as a definition of ' stone '. But the total abandonment of Aquinas's position by so many of his *soi-disant* followers in our own time cannot be called sound strategy. If we can find no class of substance-terms, such as Aquinas thought the term ' stone ' was, the concept of substance becomes pretty well useless; and things are not much better if one holds (as I have heard suggested) that just the term ' man ' is a genuine substance-term, expressing our knowledge of man's nature; for unless we have from elsewhere, from other instances, some idea of what it is for a term to signify a kind of material substance, we shall not really know what we are doing in ascribing this character to the rather peculiar term ' man '.

A first step towards understanding Aquinas is to reject the
H

Lockean thesis that there is no nominal essence of individuals. The very weak reasons given for this thesis—e.g. that one cannot tell from the mere sound of the name which sort of individual it is used to refer to—might well arouse our suspicion. Moreover, it is clear that someone who overheard a conversation containing the name ' Chuckery ', but did not gather whether this was the name of a person, a city, or a river, would be uncomprehending in the same way as if he had misconstructed which sort of term one of the general terms used in the conversation was. A proper name is used in order to keep on referring to one and the same thing of a given kind—the same man or city or river.

This brings us, not yet to the notion of a substantial term, but at least to that of a *substantival* term. Aquinas calls out attention to a feature of Latin grammar—that substantives are singular or plural on their own account, whereas adjectives ' agree in number ' with substantives. This suggests to him a logical distinction between two sorts of terms: substantival terms, to which the question ' how many?' applies directly, and adjectival terms, to which this question applies only in so far as they are used to add a qualification to substantival terms. One may ask how many cats there are in a room: but not, how many black things there are in the room; only, how many black *cats* (say) there are in the room. The basis of this distinction is that the sense of ' cat ' determines a sense for ' one and the same cat ', whereas the sense of ' black thing ' does not in the least determine what shall count as one and the same black thing. Frege was obscurely aware of this peculiarity of ' adjectival ' terms—he remarks that in such cases no *finite* number is assignable; but of course, so long as we confine ourselves to an ' adjectival ' term, *no* number is assignable; it is not that we never come to an end of counting, but that we cannot even begin, since there is no criterion for whether a black thing is the same black thing as one already counted. (Cf. here Ia q. 39 art. 3 and Frege's *Grundlagen* § 54.)

Not every substantival term is a substantial term—neither ' city ' nor ' river ' stands for a kind of substance. But what is further to be noticed as regards substantival terms generally is that none of them is a mere conjunction of independent non-substantival terms. A term like ' red square ' does not stand for an identifiable kind of thing; *nec vere ens, nec vere unum;* ' one and the same—' makes no better sense when prefixed to a conjunction of ' adjectival ' terms than when prefixed to a single one. (We may here observe that Aquinas's use of '*unum*', ' one , in the topic-neutral or ' transcendental' sense is often best understood by an English paraphrase using the expression ' identical' or ' (one and) the same '.) And ' black cat ' stands for an identifiable kind of thing only because ' cat ' does so; ' one and the same black cat' means ' one and the same cat (which incidentally is black) '. Similarly ' one and the same postman ' means ' one and the same man (who incidentally collects and delivers the mail) '. In general: any substantival term that is (analysable as) a conjunction of independent terms must contain as one member of the conjunction another substantival term; and so in the end we must get to a substantival term that *merely* signifies a certain form or nature, without any added qualifications.

From this there follows the unreasonableness of accounting for ostensible substance-words in a Lockian way. Such a term as ' man ' or ' cat ' or ' gold ' certainly does not stand for a mere congeries of properties; for this would afford no rationale for *counting* men or cats or *identifying* a parcel of gold. One might try saying that the congeries of properties would all belong to one and the same *substance* in each case—that ' substance ' itself would be the substantival term here involved. But it is a fantastic idea that e.g. the number of cats in a room should be determinable by identifying the several substances in the room and then picking out from among them the ones that had the congeries of properties signified by the word ' cat '.

It may thus seem reasonable to hold that in many cases ' substance ' terms are genuinely such—genuinely express our ability to recognise the natures or quiddities of material things. To be sure, we need not suppose that men ordinarily know how to *define* such terms; they may only know their meaning as the meaning of ' square ' is known before studying geometry. Nor need we suppose that the sorting-out of things into natural kinds is an infallible operation. But Locke's fear that a scientific classification of things would not at all correspond to our ordinary classification has not been verified; chemists do not now ' in vain seek for the same qualities in one parcel of sulphur, antimony, or vitriol which they have found in others '; and Locke's inference that these chemical terms stand for mere collocations of obvious sensible properties, not for ' precise, distinct, real essences ', was accordingly ill-founded. In fact, of course, the troubles he refers to were due to variable amounts of impurity of various sorts, and the chemists did not conclude, as he would have had them do, that 'sulphur', 'antimony', etc., were vague terms answering to no scientifically determinable reality, but set about devising techniques of purification. As regards natural kinds in the animate world, Locke's scepticism was largely based on a credulous acceptance of old wives' tales: about rational parrots, and about 'monsters' or 'changelings' produced by the intercourse of bulls with mares, cats with rats, and 'drills' with women. It is worth mentioning that Mill's remarks on natural kinds exhibit the fundamental good sense which the prejudices he inherited could not always obscure (see his *Logic*, I. vii. 4, III. xxii).

(3) *Esse*. I shall leave this term untranslated because no single word is a good English equivalent. People who render it by 'being' will generally be found to be using the same word for the quite different term '*ens*', which does not make for clarity; the same is true of French writers who talk about '*l'être*'. In Aquinas, *ens* is *that which* 'is' (*quod est*) and *esse* is *that by which* a thing 'is' (*quo est*): this is a case—or rather an analogical extension—of the distinction between *quod* and *quo* that we have just been studying. We must therefore first find out how Aquinas is here using the verb 'est', 'is', or 'exists'.

On the role of this verb, Aquinas's views underwent a change. In his earlier writings (e.g. in *De Ente et Essentia*) he sought to establish a real distinction between the *esse* of a given thing and its nature or essence from the obvious difference in meaning between the questions '*an est*?', 'is there such a thing?', and '*quid est*?', 'what nature of thing is it?' Later on, however, though he retained the doctrine of there being a real distinction between *esse* and nature or essence, he explicitly repudiated this way of establishing it, and explained that what he meant by *esse* had nothing to do with the existence that is asserted by affirmative answers to the question '*an est*?'

This change of view has been ignored by most commentators; it will be good to consider a few texts that place it beyond doubt. The clearest ones relate to the 'existence' of privations like blindness. Blindness is not an *ens* and has no *esse*; for it is not among the things that are, being on the contrary precisely the absence of what would be an existing thing, viz the absence of sight from an eye. All the same, we can truly say that *there is* blindness in a given eye, which is an affirmative answer to an '*an est*?' question. Thus the existence asserted in this case by saying ' there is . . . ' is quite different from Aquinas's *esse*. (Ia q. 48 art. 2 ad 2 um.)

Again, Aquinas holds that God's nature and God's *esse* are identical. On the view that the distinction between nature and *esse* is to be explained in terms of the difference in meaning between the questions ' *quid est?* ' and ' *an est?* ' this would commit him to saying that in God's case the two questions have the very same answer— that to know or state that God exists is the same thing as knowing or stating what God is. People are indeed prepared to defend this consequence; but it is no wonder that Aquinas shrank from it, and abandoned the view that would commit him to it; for it is clearly nonsensical, as may be shown by the following imaginary dialogue:

Theist. There is a God.

Atheist. So *you* say: but what sort of being is this God of yours?

Theist. Why, I've just told you! *There is a* God; *that*'s what God is!

Attacks have sometimes been made on modern symbolic logic because it prevents people who take it seriously from talking the same sort of nonsense as my *Theist.* But we need not use devices of modern logic, like the quantifier-notation, to expose *Theist's* confusion; as Schopenhauer remarked, Aristotle had prophetically refuted it: ' There is nothing whose essence it is that there is such a thing, for there is no such kind of things as *things that there are* '. (*An. Post.* 92 b 13–4.)

At Ia q. 3 art. 4, ad 2 um, Aquinas actually uses the obvious difference in meaning that there would be between a statement that there is a God and a statement of what God is, a *prima facie* objection to the doctrine that God's *esse* and nature are identical. His reply to this objection is that to know (by reason of a proof) that there is a God is not to apprehend God's *esse*; God's *esse* and his nature are alike beyond our knowledge in this life; and as a positive account of the assertion that there is a God, he tells us that this ' existence ' consists in the truth of an affirmative predication (*compositio*). ' God exists ' is true if and only if *the term* ' God ' is affirmatively predicable. In other words: To say that there is a God is true, not because some attribute signified by ' there is ' belongs to God, but because Divine attributes belong to something or other; just as blindness ' exists ' in that ' blind ' is truly predicable of some eyes, not because blindness has the attribute of existing. This view is clearly correct, and a firm grasp of it will enable us to steer through all the shoals of the Cartesian Ontological Argument.

To cite just one more text: Aquinas teaches that Christ has not two *esses*, as God and as man, because a Divine Person with one *esse* and a man with another *esse* would be distinct persons, and to assert a distinction of persons in Christ is heretical. We are not here concerned with the dogmatic theology of this idea, but only with the fact that Aquinas brusquely dismisses the objection that there must be two *esses* in Christ because there being a God is different from there being a man: this ' there being ', he says, has nothing to do with the case, for in the same way we can speak of ' there being ' blindness, where there is no *esse* at all. (*Quodlibet* IX, q. 2, art. 3.) Once again, Aquinas has clearly decided that what he refers to as *esse* is not the ' existence ' signified by ' there is a . . . '.

Aquinas's conception of *esse* thus depends on there being a sense of the verb ' *est* ' or ' is ' quite other than the ' there is ' sense. We need to recognise a certain ambiguity of the verb ' is ', and of corresponding verbs in other Indo-European languages, which has led to endless philosophical puzzles and fallacies. Thus, Parmenides argued: ' There is no time: for otherwise it will follow that there is something besides what is ': ' it neither was nor will be, for it is now all together '. Again, there is a riddle in Plutarch's life of Alexander the Great: 'Are there more living or dead?—Living: for the dead are not '. The answer to the riddle is clearly a logical trick, and Parmenides was clearly playing the same trick upon himself unawares.

We may express the difference between the two senses of ' is ' as follows: An individual may be said to ' be ', meaning that it is at present actually existing; on the other hand, when we say that ' there is ' an X (where ' X ' goes proxy for a general term), we are saying concerning a kind or description of things, Xs, that there is at least one thing of that kind or description. ' The dead are not ' is true in the sense that any proper name that yields a true statement when it replaces ' x ' in ' x is dead ' will also turn ' x is no more ' into a true statement; but it is false if it is taken in the sense that no predication of the form ' x is dead ' is true. Frege was clear as to this distinction, though he rightly had no special interest, as a *mathematical* logician, in assertions of present actuality. It is great misfortune that Russell has dogmatically reiterated that the ' there is ' sense of the 'substantive' verb 'to be' is the only one that logic can recognise as legitimate; for the other meaning—present actuality —is of enormous importance in philosophy, and only harm can be done by a Procrustean treatment which either squeezes assertions of present actuality into the 'there is' form of lops them off as non-sensical.

It is the present-actuality sense of 'est' that is involved in Aquinas's discussions of *ens* and *esse*. It corresponds to the uses of the verb 'to exist' in which we say that an individual thing comes to exist, continues to exist, ceases to exist, or again to the uses of 'being' in which we say that a thing is brought into being or kept in being by another thing. For the sort of things that are animate, 'to be' in this sense has the same application as 'to be alive': *vivere viventibus est esse*. Thus a dead man is said not to be, or to be no more: 'Joseph is not, and Simeon is not'. Contrariwise, Homer speaks of the Gods who 'ever are' i.e. live for ever.

The difficulty may be raised that if 'Joseph is not' is true, that 'Joseph' no longer has anything to refer to, so there is no longer anything to make a statement about. But it is quite a different thing for a name still to have refeence rand for the thing named to be still in existence; the significant use of a demonstrative sometimes requires the actual existence—indeed, the actual presence—of the thing pointed to, but there is no such restriction on the use of proper names. Even among present-tense predicates, some imply the present existence of the thing named by the subject (e.g. 'sees' and 'is in love') while others do not (e.g. 'is admired' or 'is an ancestor of so-and-so'); and there is no neat logical rule for sorting out which are which—but why should there be? (What may obstruct the acceptance of these obvious points are certain deep prejudices about meaning. Cf. Wittgenstein's *Philosophical Investigations*, §§ 37–45.)

Now when we were discussing form we saw that for Aquinas there would be no such thing as simply being, or continuing to be, 'the same': what is meant by a thing's continuing to be 'the same' would be its continuing to be the X, where 'X' is some general, predicable, term standing for a form or nature. Similarly, there is no such thing as a thing's *just* going on existing; when we speak of this, we must always really be referring to some form or nature, X, such that for that thing to go on existing is for it to go on being X. (For a man to go on existing is for him to go on being a man—one and the same man; for a statue to go on existing is for it to go on being the same shape; etc.) *Esse*, therefore, is always related to some form or other; and any persistent *esse* is the continued existence of some individualized form.

'The same matter' constitutes an apparent exception to this; but we must remember that here it is not that something continues to be the same matter, but that the same matter continues or begins or ceases to be a thing of a given kind, and the *esse* comes and goes with the form that characterizes a thing of that kind. The phrase 'the same matter' is in any event a special case, because 'matter' as we saw is not a general term predicable of pieces of matter.

So far, apart from throwing light on some uses of the substantive verb 'to be', Aquinas's doctrine of *esse* really adds nothing over and above his doctrine of form. The plurality of *esse*s that Aquinas asserts there is in a given individual thing simply corresponds to the plurality of individualized forms. There is no 'continuing to exist' that is not something's continuing to be so-and-so—to be a man, to be red, to be round—and 'that whereby' the something is so-and-so is always an individualized form—an individual human soul, redness, or shape. We may say that these individualized forms differ in respect of *esse*, because there may be a 'continuing to exist' in respect of one apart from another: a body may cease to be round while remaining red, or *vice versa*, or cease to be either red or round while remaining the same kind of body.

Aquinas further maintains that each individualized form is really distinct from the corresponding *esse*—from 'that whereby' the individualized form exists. Now this is a surprising doctrine. We may perhaps recognise Socrates and the redness of Socrates' nose as individuals distinct in *esse*, because the redness of the nose comes to be and ceases to be without the same thing's happening to Socrates; but it is not at once clear why we should recognise a real distinction between the soul or individualized life 'whereby' Socrates lives and the *esse* 'whereby' he exists, and again between 'that whereby' his nose is red and the *esse* 'whereby' the redness of his nose continues to exist: the plurality of *esse*s strikes one as idly duplicating the plurality of individualized forms.

Aquinas, however, considers this doctrine necessary and fundamental; it has very many applications. One of the more interesting ways of establishing the real distinction is to consider the intensity of qualities. It is a notion taken for granted in modern science that there are all sorts of attributes in which there can be variation in degree down to zero without any transition to, or any increasing admixture of, an opposite attribute. Thus, light can vary in intensity down to zero, without changing to a different sort of light; and darkness is a mere privation, not a physical attribute. In this particular case, Aristotle reached an essentially correct view. But the *general* notion of intensity, indeed the very word, is an invention of medieval philosophy; the name is taken from a particular case of just such an attribute as varies in this way—the force of *tension* in a string. It was the lack of this notion that brought Greek science to a dead end: the Greeks tried to work with pairs of opposites suggested by ordinary language—heavy and light, right and left, hot and cold, etc.—which turned out scientifically useless. (It may be conjectured that the medievals were driven to formulate the distinct notion of intensity by theological considerations; a higher degree of God's grace could hardly be taken to mean: grace with a smaller admixture of sin!)

What Aquinas gives us is a philosophical analysis of intensive magnitude. When a thing x passes from a lower to a higher degree of the quality F, or *vice versa*, the Fness of x remains while the degree of Fness changes; there is thus a real distinction between the individ- ualized form 'whereby' x is F and the degree to which x if F. This distinction, it is interesting to note, is a 'real' one according to Hume's use of the term; Hume himself only failed to draw this conclusion because he drew instead the manifestly false one that all the degrees of a given quality are perfectly distinct from one another like different colours or tones. We can easily see that the cases are quite different. When a thing remains coloured but changes from red to green, we cannot distinguish between a quality that remains and a quality that changes; at the first, the colour of the thing just is its redness, as said before, and this quality does not remain but is replaced by another; there is no more an identifiable 'colour of this thing' that is first red and then green than there is an identifiable sovereign of Great Britain who was first a middle-aged man and then a young woman. On the other hand, the same individual quality does persist when there is only a change in intensity.

Now an increase in intensity of a quality is like a coming-to-be, a decrease in intensity like a passing-away, of that quality: e.g. a sound's suddenly becoming louder is like a sound's suddenly starting, a sound's suddenly becoming softer is like a sound's suddenly stopping. We may here compare Kant's idea that a human soul could perish by elanguescence—by all its activities' gradually diminishing in intensity to zero. Aquinas according equates the intensive magnitude of a quality with its *esse*: an increase or diminution of intensity means that this instance of the quality *exists* more or less in the bearer of the quality. And so, wherever intensive magnitude comes in, there is a real distinction between the individualized form and the *esse*. (Cf. IIa IIae q. 24 art. 4 ad 3um, art. 5 c., art. 5 ad 3um).

This argument, though relatively clear, lacks generality; for a shape, or a relation like fatherhood, or a substantial form, does not admit of differences in intensity. The other two arguments we have to consider apply to forms generally. The second argument (Ia q. 3 art. 5) is a succinct and rather puzzling one. Two men, Aquinas says, have humanity in common, and a man and a horse have animality in common; but the two men, or the two animals, have different *esse*s. What this last means is fairly easy to understand: the situation of different living things having the same *esse* would be like that in the fairy-tale, where a young man rashly shot the family cat and killed off the whole family at a stroke; by contrast to this we may say that different animals normally have different *esse*s, so that one can cease to be apart from another. But in view of Aquinas's doctrine of universals, it is hard to see the force of his saying that two men or two animals ' share in a quiddity or essence '. So far as his words go, he might well have been taken to argue that since the *esse*s are different while the quiddity is the same, the quiddity of each man or animal must differ from the *esse*—only this cannot be his mind, since for him the humanity of this man is not identical with the humanity of that man, and the animality of a man is even unlike that of a horse. We should rather, I think, construe his argument thus: ' while the quiddities (the animalities) of two animals are certainly different, this difference arises from the side not of quiddity but of *esse*; were there not difference of *esse*, there could be but one individualized animality in two animals even of different species; as there is but one individualized animality in the two kidneys of a given animal, or again in his kidney and liver, differently organized as these are '.

The third argument brings us to Aquinas's theory of thought and sense-perception. We must here observe that Aquinas's ' *intelligere* ' should be rendered ' think of ' rather than ' understand ': it is the

conventional rendering of Aristotle's νοεῖν. We may start from the
fact that we normally describe a sensation or a thought as a sensation
of X (where 'X' goes proxy for some possible description of a
physical thing by sensible attributes) or as a thought *of* Y (where 'Y'
may represent any description whatsoever that makes sense). Moreover, we are tempted to say that this is the only way a thought or
sensation can be described: this is all there is to a thought or sensation. But saying this has obvious difficulties. It seems to make the
whole being of a sensation or thought consist in a relation to something else: it is as if someone said he had a picture of a cat that was
not painted on any background or in any medium, there being
nothing to it except that it was a picture of a cat. This is hard
enough: to make matters worse, the terminus of the supposed
relation may not exist—a drunkard's 'seeing' snakes is not related
to any real snake, nor my thought of a phoenix to any real phoenix.
Philosophers have sought a way out of this difficulty by inventing
chimerical entities like 'snakish sense-data' or 'real but non-
existent phoenixes' as termini of the cognitive relation.

Aquinas's view is that redness occurring in a physical object and
in my sense-experience, or again animality occurring in a real live
animal and in my thought of an animal, do not differ on the side of
the characteristics that occur, but on the side of their *manner* of
occurrence. The individual rednesses of two different red things
differ in *esse*, as we have seen, and so do the individual animalities of
two different animals; here we have one individual redness or animality in physical nature, and another in the mind of a given man,
likewise differing in *esse*, but there is now a difference in the kind or
manner of *esse*—between *esse naturale* and *esse intentionale*, to use
Aquinas's terms. What makes a sensation or thought of an X to be
of an X is that it is an individual occurrence of that very form or
nature which occurs in an X—it is thus that our mind ' reaches right
up to the reality'; what makes it to be a *sensation or thought* of an X
rather than an actual X or an actual X-ness is that X-ness here occurs
in the special way called *esse intentionale* and not in the 'ordinary'
way called *esse naturale*. This solution resolves the difficulty. It
shows how *being of an X* is not a relation in which the thought or
sensation stands, but is simply what the thought or sensation *is*—
which is what we were tempted to say, but could not see our way clear
to saying. And there may be cases in which X-ness has only *esse*

intentionale in my mind without there being any X-ness in the physical world—but this does not mean that my mind stands in relation to a non-existent reality.

If seeing red and thinking of red alike consist in red occurring with *esse intentionale*, what then is the difference between them, or in general between sensation and thought? Aquinas's reply is that thinking of red is a *non-material* occurrence of redness (*esse immateriale*). Sensations occur under the spatio-temporal conditions of the material world. The time taken by sensations (as also by mental images, feelings, etc.) is that time which is measured by the local motion of bodies, e.g. of the hands on a dial; and again, the ' doubling ' of a sensation (or image) is like that ' being in two bits ' which, as we saw, is for Aquinas an attribute of physical things (a species of ' discrete quantity '). But thought, Aquinas holds, occurs in discrete pulses which are indivisible: the thought that the pack of cards is on the table occurs all at once or not at all, and though it has some sort of correlation with such a physical process as the words in which I express it, it does not occur in physical time, either at an instant or over a period. (What sort of ideas the contrary view leads to may be seen from William James's fantasy: that the thought lasts for the whole time of the sentence ' the pack of cards is on the table ', and goes through successive phases, in which bits of the thought corresponding to the successive words are prominent— including bits corresponding to ' the ' and ' of '.) And again, if I *think of* two pennies, there is no such ' doubleness ' in my thought as there is in my seeing or imagining if I *see or visualise* two pennies.

Aquinas accordingly holds that a thought consists in the *non-material* occurrence of a form or nature—an occurrence apart from matter and material conditions. There can on this view be no special nature of the thought-process, to be discovered empirically; such a special nature might be expected to impose restrictions on what can be thought of, as coloured glass does on what can be seen through it —and Aquinas regards this sort of restriction as evidently impossible. Whatever nature of thing an A may be, if there can be an A there can be a thought of an A. (We must not be misled into accepting this principle because of the impossibility of giving a counter-example, since the counter-example would itself have been thought of: that would be no proof at all, and Aquinas makes no appeal to it.) For if it is not impossible for there to be something of the nature A, then there can be something of that nature existing with *esse naturale*, and equally there can be something of that nature existing with *esse intentionale*. Something of the nature A existing with *esse naturale* is an actual A; something of that nature existing with *esse intentionale* is a sensation or thought of an A. But the 'material conditions' under which sensation occurs exclude a universal capacity for sensation of all natures of things that can exist: it is only when the *esse* is not merely intentional, but also freed from the limitations of matter, that we have an unrestricted possibility for the occurrence, by that kind of *esse*, of whatever natures can occur in reality at all.

The view that thought has a special, empirically discoverable, character naturally goes with the idea of a special sort of cognitive power whereby one's own thoughts come to one's notice: sometimes this is supposed to be *sui generis* and referred to by such terms as 'consciousness' or 'reflection'; sometimes it is assimilated to the senses that acquaint us with external events, and regarded as a sort of inner vision (intro-spection) or inner feeling. For Aquinas, however, a thought (or a movement of the will, which shall be discussed when we come on to *Operations and Tendencies*) exists in a mind with *esse intentionale*; and since that very sort of *esse* constitutes a thing's being thought of, a thought (or movement of the will) is thought of in the very same act as the object that is thought of (or willed). That is, it is thought of in a way; for a deliberate reflection about something that passes in one's mind is of course a new thought. But there is no place in Aquinas's account for a special means whereby one's own thoughts may come to one's ken; a thought is as it were self-luminous or transparent to itself—in Aquinas's phrase, it is 'an actual intelligible', i.e. it is thought of in virtue of its very existence or *esse*.

On this view of thought, one may well wonder at the fact that thought can occur in a corporeal creature like man; and some of Aquinas's contemporaries, who shared his view of thought, held that what really thinks is not a man but a single incorporeal intelligence that somehow manifests itself through all the many human organisms. Aquinas held that it *is* a man who thinks, but that this thinking is predicable only of his soul, not of his body.

Here a number of difficulties arise. First, I think we must allow that the traditional way of speaking, in which a man is said to consist of soul *and* body, does not fit in well with Aquinas's thought, and that he creates obscurity by continuing to talk in this way. A man is an animal, and an animal is a body; so a man *is* a body, not a body *plus* something else. Again, for Aquinas, Socrates is a man, and is an animal, and is a body (sc. a *single* body), by virtue of one and the same individualized form, Socrates' soul or individual life; so ' Socrates' body ' already involves the individualized form that makes it a (single) body, Socrates' soul; so we cannot reckon Socrates' body and soul *together* as parts of Socrates, in any acceptable sense of ' part '. Again, the body and soul are not parts into which a man can be dissolved: even if the soul can exist disembodied, a dead man not only is not a man, but is not even *a* body (rather, it is now a loose congeries of bodies). What remains after death is not the same *body* but the same *stuff* or *matter*; similarly, we must say that at any given time a man consists of an individual life (the soul) in a certain portion of *materia prima*—not: in a body.

It is easy, however, to rephrase Aquinas's account of what it is that thinks. A man thinks in virtue of his soul—in virtue of having that specific sort of life. Further, we cannot identify his thinking with any process that goes on for a definite time in a definite region of his body; still less can there be a bodily organ of thought. Sensations, mental images, and feelings, which by their nature occur under the conditions of matter, positively require bodily organs; and Aquinas thinks it impossible that they should occur in a disembodied mind, and consequently, that there should be any incorporeal existence of the souls of animals, which he regards as capable of sentience only, not of thought. (Likewise, conversely, wicked spirits in hell cannot suffer from any aches and pains, but only from the thwarting of their evil will.) And thus the sensations and mental images that subserve the ends of thought and supply it with materials can have location, say ' in the middle part of the brain ' (as Aquinas says); but such brain-processes, the like of which may also occur in a parrot that can talk, are not neural correlates of *thought*.

The immaterial nature of thought naturally raises the question whether the human soul is capable of disembodied existence; Aquinas asserts this capability, but frankly faces the obvious difficulties that arise on his premises. (1) If the human soul is an individualized form existing in a certain animal, how can it survive the death of that animal? How can the individual life of an animal go on when the animal no longer is alive? (2) Again, if different men simultaneously existing are distinct by consisting of different parcels of matter, then their souls are distinguishable only in view of this fact; and then how can the souls remain distinct when disembodied? (3) What are disembodied souls to think about, since without a body they cannot have the data of sense or the help of imagination?

(1) To understand Aquinas's reply to this difficulty, we must understand that for him it is not only a necessary, but also a sufficient, condition for the occurrence of thought that there should be an individualized form existing otherwise than in matter. Accordingly, he tells us that if there could be the substantial form of a loaf of bread existing apart from the bread, it would exist as a form that was *thought of*, and that (since this thought would occur apart from anything else in which it inhered) this individualized form would exist in *its own thought of itself*. The *esse* of the form would thus be *naturale* and *intentionale* at once; this does not imperil the distinction between a thought of an X and an actual X, for what is required for that distinction is that an *esse need* not be at once *esse naturale* and *esse intentionale*, not that it *cannot* be both at once. Now as regards the persistence of the individualized form of a loaf after the loaf has ceased to be, this argument is intended as a *reductio ad absurdum*: for since a loaf is inanimate, its form does not admit of being the subject of any thinking activity. (IIIa q. 75 art. 6.) But the embodied soul of a man can be a thinking subject; and so, Aquinas thinks, it can also exist apart from matter with an *esse* at once *naturale* and *intentionale*— in its own thought of itself.

(2) Aquinas holds that each disembodied human soul would remain individualized, because at any time there would be a certain determinate parcel of matter such that, if at that time the soul came to be the form of that matter, there must again be the very man whose soul the soul was. *This* soul is tailor-made (*commensurata*) for reunion to *this* parcel of matter; we must hold that its very nature contains such a capacity for union—otherwise we should be regarding union to a body as a mere external or accidental relation in which a soul stands, which is contrary to Aquinas's whole doctrince of the soul. (*Contra Gentes* IIc. 85.)

(3) Aquinas regards the need for thought to be supported by sensuous or imaginative experience as one that no longer exists for a disembodied soul. While in the body, the soul can actually think

only by the help of sense and imagination, which are processes belonging to the physical order; this is because the soul, as the form of a body, itself in a way belongs to the physical order; and accordingly anything that interrupts or disturbs the flow of sensuous and imaginative experience (sleep, drugs, brain lesions, etc.) will interrupt or disturb the flow of thought. But a disembodied soul is no longer liable to such physical influences. It does not follow that it will no longer be able to think; as McTaggart said, the fact that toothache may make consecutive thought impossible has no tendency to show that you cannot think when the tooth is extracted.

The disembodied soul will retain the purely intelligible or logical, though not the sensuous, content of its earthly thoughts.—The distinction that Aquinas wishes to draw is certainly in a sense valid: e.g. the same imagery may answer to very different thoughts, and the same thought be served by very various imagery. What is difficult is to conceive of thought as continuing without any sensuous content at all.

Further, the disembodied soul is itself literally a living image of other disembodied souls; it is a likeness of them, existing with *esse intentionale* as well as *esse naturale*; and this, for Aquinas, is a sufficient condition of these other souls' coming to its ken.

This description of the life that would be possible for disembodied souls is meagre and unattractive; but why should it be otherwise? Why should philosophy be expected to give more than a very sketchy and abstract account of what disembodied existence could be like? It may well be protested that a soul whose thoughts have no sensuous content, and whose rational choices are unaccompanied by the familiar warm human feelings, cannot be *I*. Aquinas would simply accept this result: *anima mea non est ego*, my departed soul is not I. It will not be *I* who live after my death unless my soul is again united to that parcel of matter for union to which it is adapted. But the question ' If a *man* die, shall *he* live again? ' is one that philosophy cannot answer in the proper sense of the question—though the Christian (and Pharisaic) doctrine of resurrection would yield an affirmative answer. As for the unattractiveness of the prospects disclosed by mere philosophy, philosophy can no more guarantee that we shall be happy hereafter than here; what in fact happens to the souls of the dead, Aquinas would say, is God's concern, and we know of it only as much as he chooses to reveal.

(4) *Operations and tendencies.* For ' operations ' Aquinas uses the corresponding Latin word, and also ' *actiones* ' and (where the context removes ambiguity) ' *actus* '; for ' tendency ' his word is ' *inclinatio* ' or ' *appetitus* '.

The notion of operations is closely bound up with that of identifiable things of a kind. As Aquinas says, what *is* a thing of a given kind is what *performs the operations* of that kind of thing (*illud est una quaeque res quod operatur operationes illius rei*). To recognise the persistent identity of a thing, we must be able to pick out from the general flux of events the contribution made by that thing's operations; we must be able to distinguish what the thing does from what merely happens to it.

At this point, unluckily, Aquinas's illustrations are a hindrance, for they are practically all vitiated by obsolete science. We are told that a stone falls downward ' naturally ' but that its motion when thrown is ' constrained ' (*violentus*); and on the other hand that the tidal movement of the sea is again ' natural ', because it is ' natural ' for water to be influenced by the Moon. Apart from this difficulty, we are all considerably affected by Humian ideas of causality, consciously or unconsciously, and this constitutes a serious barrier between us and Aquinas. I shall try to do a little towards removing this barrier, and to show the need for ideas corresponding to Aquinas's idea of operation and tendency even on the basis of modern science.

Since Hume, the opinion had been widely held that the task of science is to establish uniformities of the form ' every event of the kind P is followed by an event of the kind Q ' or ' any event of the kind Q is preceded by an event of the kind P '. To be sure, the progress of science has brought into prominence ' uniformities ' in which the attributes of the earlier and the later event are not determinately specified, but instead the one attribute is asserted to stand in a definite functional relation to the other; however, for our present purpose this makes little difference. It would still be held that science aims at establishing uniformities which are, so far as we can see, merely matters of fact: we have no intuitive insight as to which propositions of this kind hold good, but must proceed inductively. The only issue between an out-and-out Humian and (say) McTaggart or Kneale would be this: are *de facto* uniformities the end of the matter; or are there natural necessities, entailments of one fact by

another, which we may have good empirical reason to believe in
even though we lack intuitive understanding of them?

This opinion, I think, is radically wrong: the laws that scientists
aim at establishing are not *de facto* uniformities, either necessary or
contingent. For any alleged uniformity is defeasible by something's
interfering and preventing the effect; to assert the uniformity as a
fact is to commit oneself to a rash judgment that such interference
never has taken place and never will. Scientists do not try to describe
natural events in terms of what always happens. Rather, certain
natural agents—bodies of certain natures—are brought into the
description, and we are told what behaviour is proper to this set of
bodies in these circumstances. If such behaviour is not realized, the
scientist looks for a new, interfering agent that has not so far been
brought into the account; this is how men discovered the planet
Neptune and the rare elements that ordinarily occur only as impurities
in other substance.

' It will happen this way unless something interferes' may sound
like the vacuous prediction 'it will happen this way unless it does
not'. But this very impression of its vacuousness is due to Humian
prejudice. A vacuous expectation can in no wise guide further
research; but if an expectation of the type 'it will happen this way
unless something interferes' is disappointed, this leads to an—often
successful—attempt to find the interfering agent.

Such interference just cannot be logically brought into a uniformity doctrine of causality—even though many people who have
held such a doctrine have talked about interference. Mill, for example,
supposes that we can account for interference by stating (a) the several
laws for the effects of several causes; (b) laws for the combination of
effects like the parallelogram law. For the effects that are said to be
produced and then combined are in fact not produced at all; the
so-called combination is alone physically real. Let us suppose that a
certain room would have its temperature raised 25° F. in an hour
by a heating unit A, and lowered 10° F. in an hour by a refrigerating
unit B; then even if in the presence of both A and B the room-
temperature rises by $(25-10)°$ F., i.e. by $15°$F., this rise of temperature,
which has happened, is certainly not compounded of a non-existent
rise of temperature by 25° F. and a non-existent fall of temperature
by 10° F. Because of interference, what on the Humian view 'always
happens' very often doesn't happen. Mill retreats into saying that

physical laws do not state what *does* happen, but what *would failing interference* happen; but this is to abandon the Humian position.

Mill is in fact pushed by the facts (*quasi ab ipsa veritate coactus*) into saying 'All laws of causation, in consequence of their liability to be counteracted, require to be stated in words affirmative of tendencies only'. It is clear from the context that Mill's use of ' tendency ' here has nothing to do with what usually happens; for he says that *all* heavy bodies *tend* to fall, although balloons do not usually fall. Similarly, he is not speaking of what is likely to happen; for, to take another of his examples, there is not the least likelihood that a one-ton pull will raise a body weighing three tons. A tendency is indeed specifiable, always and exclusively, by describing what happens if the tendency is fulfilled; but not all tendencies do pass to fulfilment, as we readily see if we refuse to muddle ourselves with talk about a ' sum of effects ', as Mill did. (He was even ready to say that if nothing happens at all, this nothing may be the ' sum ' of *actual effects* that are equal and opposite!) We must rather say: Given the natural agents involved, we know their tendencies; given all the tendencies involved, we know what will actually happen. (Thus, given the members of a structure, we know what stresses will be set up; and given all the stresses, we know what deformations will be produced.)

This doctrine of tendencies, which we find in Mill's *Logic* all mixed up with an entirely incompatible Humian invariable-succession theory, is very close indeed to Aquinas's doctrine of *inclinationes* or *appetitus* in nature; and we may therefore suitably borrow the word ' tendency ' to express Aquinas's notion. As I said, Aquinas was almost wholly wrong as to the actual examples of natural tendency that he gave; but this need not disturb us. For he would insist that describing natural effects in terms of tendencies is not a speculative philosopher's hypothesis as to how things aim at a good arrangement —it is the only way we can describe natural effects at all; and the errors in his own statements of natural tendencies do not matter. Socrates in the *Phaedo* blamed Anaxagoras for trying to explain natural processes in terms of ' vapour, ether, water, and the like nonsense ' rather than in terms of how things *ought* to be; Aquinas would not in the least object to Anaxagoras' type of explanation, but would say that such explanation would *ipso facto* ascribe natural tendencies to vapour, ether, water, etc.—otherwise it could not even characterize their behaviour.

We must be careful not to regard natural tendencies as mere potentialities. For, first, there are often potentialities in a situation in which, given the agents actually present, there is no corresponding tendency. A piece of soft wax in London has the potentiality of assuming any number of shapes, but it has no particular tendency to take e.g. the shape of a Birmingham man's thumbprint. Again, if tendencies are to be regarded as mere potentialities, then what actually happens will be the resultant of a lot of things that would happen if only there were not other things that would happen if . . . and at that rate nothing would ever actually happen, just as no consent is actually obtainable from the firm of Spenlow and Jorkens when each of them *would* consent if only his partner would. A tendency for something to happen is different from its actually happening; but yet a tendency is somehow actual, not a mere potentiality, a ' would happen if '.

Even though the other tendencies involved in a given situation prevent the actual fulfilment of a given tendency, its presence will always make a difference to what actually happens; and the procedure of scientific explanation is to infer natural tendencies from what actually happens, and then predict what will happen from the natural tendencies of the agents believed to be operative. This procedure demands either the physical isolation of agents or the mental analysis of their joint result. What characterizes a given kind of natural agent is not so much actual operations as tendencies; but some tendencies come into effect to a recognisable extent in spite of inter-ference—otherwise we could never discern any tendencies at all, since a tendency is specifiable only by the operation to which it is a tendency. On the other hand, conversely, operations of a thing are distinguished from what merely happens to it by being fulfilment of its own tendencies.

Aquinas maintains that every tendency proceeds from what a thing *is*; a thing acts, or at least tends to act, the way it *is*—to use his frequent example (scientifically dubious as it is), fire tends to heat things because it is hot. It is not too difficult to bring this up-to-date: if we have an expression for the rate of temperature-change of a body in a room where there are bodies of various temperatures, reflecting powers, etc., this expression will present a sum of various terms depending on these attributes of the bodies, and each term will express a tendency, an *appetitus naturalis*.

We must now consider operations and tendencies that proceed, not from forms existing with *esse naturale* like the temperature of a body, but from forms whose *esse* is intentional. First, we can now supplement what was said, under the heading of *esse*, about sensation and thought. Aquinas holds that the actual occurrence of a sensation or a thought is not constituted by a form, existing with *esse intentionale*, which is a sensible or intelligible likeness (*species*) of the thing apprehended: actual sensation or actual thinking is rather an operation proceeding from that form, as the act of heating proceeds from the form of heat. The point of this distinction is clear for *intelligible* likenesses. There is an obvious difference between possessing a concept and actually exercising that concept in one's thinking; and Aquinas's philosophical account of this difference is that mere possession of a concept consists in an intelligible likeness of the thing conceived, whereas the exercise of the concept is an operation proceeding from that likeness—both the operation and the intelligible likeness from which it proceeds having *esse intentionale* in a man's mind. But it is far less obvious why we should distinguish between the act of sensation and the sensible likeness, existing intentionally in the sense-faculty, from which the act proceeds; and there arise here some difficult controversies, which I must pass over.

These operations of sense and thought are 'fulfilments of tendencies' only in a rather weak, extended, meaning of the term; for at that rate any exercise of a capacity is a 'fulfilment of tendency'; moreover, the goal of the ' tendency ' is the generation or employment of a likeness that exists intentionally within the agent, not anything whose existence would be *esse naturale*. We get a significantly new case, however, when the tendency, although it arises from an agent's (sensuous or intellectual) apprehension of something, is directed towards or away from something that would exist *otherwise* than in the agent's apprehensions—with *esse naturale*. It is here that Aquinas finds a place for animal desires and emotions, and for the will.

Aquinas says there would be no need to employ a notion of animal appetite as distinct from the natural tendencies of an animal, if all of an animal's activities were directed towards producing sensations in the animal itself; for it belongs to the nature of an animal to be sensitive, so there would on this supposition be ' fulfilment of tendencies ' only in the degenerate sense in which any exercise of a capacity 'fulfils a tendency'. In fact, however, it is manifest that animals' activities have as goals the production of physical states of affairs like nutrition, growth, and reproduction, and the avoidance of physical harm, and not only the production or avoidance of sensations. Aquinas holds that such activities show forth a special sort of tendency, animal appetite; which proceeds from the animal's apprehending in some way the goal of the tendency, i.e. what the tendency is directed towards or away from. It is this origination from an apprehension of the goal that is characteristic of animal appetite; that the appetite is *felt* by the animal is something consequential. Since the appetite arises from an apprehension on the animal's part, it itself shares in the *esse intentionale* belonging to the animal's apprehension; but to exist with *esse intentionale* in an animal's sense-faculties is what Aquinas holds to constitute: being an object of the animal's sensitive awareness—being felt.

Many psychologists of the present day hold that men are moved, in the last resort, only by ' drives ' that they share with the lower animals; all that is distinctively human being a complication of means and manners of satisfying these ' drives ', due to the greater complexity of the human mind. Aquinas would regard this opinion as highly unreasonable. Animal appetite is tendency originating in an animal's sense-apprehensions; but man can envisage all sorts of things outside the compass of animal apprehensions, and it is not reasonable to suppose that only such apprehensions can give rise in man to a tendency towards or away from the thing apprehended. A man can, for instance, envisage the possession of a bank-balance; and this apprehension, which is wholly beyond the scope of the lower animals, can give rise to a money-getting tendency. The characteristic insatiability of some human desires, like avarice, arises on Aquinas's view from the potential infinity of the apprehended goal, say the possession of wealth; and here again, animals are incapable of apprehending such a goal—they cannot, like Cecil Rhodes, think of the inaccessible riches of the Moon and be saddened by the thought.

A tendency proceeding from a *rational* or *intellectual* apprehension of the goal is what Aquinas regards as constituting will or volition. That men are *aware* of what they will is for him a consequential feature of will, just as it is a consequential feature of animal appetite that it is *felt*; for, in virtue of its origin in a rational apprehension, the tendency that constitutes will has intelligible *esse* in the mind, i.e. it is thought of. But Aquinas does not reach the notion of will by any such means as inviting us to attend to a peculiar quality of consciousness that attends e.g. the movement of our arms and legs and tongues.

We can best understand Aquinas's doctrine of will if we contrast it with Hume's—' by the will, I mean nothing but the internal impression we feel and are conscious of, when we knowingly give rise to any new motion of the body, or new perception of the mind '. Waiving difficulties that might arise from the very notion of an ' internal impression ', we can see that in any event such an ' impression ' must be irrelevant; for the phrase ' knowingly give rise to ' already suffices to characterize voluntariness, whether or not an ' internal impression ' is present. Now this phrase, on the face of it, refers to a sort of causality—and a sort that Hume, on his own principles, has no right to recognise. He proceeds to deal with the causality of will on the same lines as other causality: we experience a regular succession in which the ' internal impression ' of will is followed by the event willed, but have no insight into the rationale of this succession, etc., etc. But if in Hume's definition of will the words ' when we knowingly give rise to ' were replaced by ' on occasions immediately preceding ', the oddity of such an account would be apparent. It is just a philosopher's sleight of hand: the words ' knowingly give rise to ' make the reader accept Hume's formula as a definition of will, and then Hume ignores these words, which are essential, and concentrates on the ' internal impression '.

For Aquinas, willing essentially consists, not in a peculiar quality of experience, but precisely in the peculiar sort of causality expressed by ' knowingly give rise to '. A voluntary act takes place as the fulfilment of a tendency that arises from the agent's consideration of the goal of the tendency. For this reason Aquinas regards it as logically impossible to coerce a man's will—to ensure that he will do something, by means outside his own control, and yet leave his doing of it voluntary. For this would mean that those tendencies which one and the same act took place as fulfilling *both* were wholly the tendencies of things outside the agent's control, *and* included tendencies arising from his own rational considerations: or, more simply, that he both had and had not a real choice how to act.

It is natural to object that volition cannot be explained solely in terms of (physical or mental) voluntary action; for volition may be thwarted—one may try and fail. So must not successful actions consist in an effect preceded by the experience of trying for that effect—of volition? Only of course, it will not be *called* trying if it succeeds—just as treason that prospers is not called treason. And this would bring us back to Hume's starting-point. The proper reply, I think, is not to quibble over the use of ' try ', but to observe that to try to do something is always actually to do something else: e.g. to try to write with numbed fingers is actually to seize and move the pen, to try to remember a name is actually to run over associations of the name in one's mind. The question ' How did he try? in what did his trying actually consist? ' always arises, and must be answered by mentioning an act—a *voluntary* act. If we held that *every* voluntary act must be preceded by ' trying ' to perform it, we should get a vicious regress; on the contrary, we must stop somewhere, with an act that the agent simply can do, and does not try to do, but just does. What makes one voluntary act to be an attempt to perform a different voluntary act must be judged from the whole context, not from an experience of trying.

The inadequacy of the account: volition followed by action comes out clearly when we consider voluntary omissions—which Aquinas often does consider, and which moral theorists often oddly neglect. Suppose a nephew is moved to keep silence, as his uncle approaches a deadly peril, by the thought of a rich inheritance; the uncle's fate is determined conjointly by the natural tendencies of the natural agents in the situation (including himself considered as a physical body), and by a tendency arising within the nephew from the consideration of the inheritance, and directed towards that inheritance (rather than a tendency towards shouting, arising from a consideration that the uncle's life is precious). The nephew's ' causing ' his uncle's death thus falls within Aquinas's general account of causality in terms of tendency.

In a way, voluntary causality is causality *par excellence*. The tendencies of natural agents like stones are not accompanied by, let alone their proceeding from, any apprehension by the agent of the goal of the tendency; in animals such apprehension is indeed inchoate, but they do not apprehend their actions as means to a goal. An agent is master (*dominus*) of its own action in so far as the tendency to action proceeds from an apprehension both of the goal and of the action as a possible means to the goal. Aquinas holds that non-voluntary causality and tendency is always derivative and subordinate to the voluntary; he illustrates the nature of this subordination by the arrow that flies according to its own way of moving to a goal determined by the archer, and by the adze that cuts wood naturally and shapes a bed because the carpenter so wields it.

II

In proving the existence of God, Aquinas shows a certain distaste for what may be called philosophical-sounding arguments—e.g. arguments based on our having an idea of a greatest or most perfect being, or on the existence of truth (e.g. in mathematics) that is contemplated by, but is not the private possession of, the individual human mind. He chooses rather to start with a notion more familiar to ordinary believers in God—that God made the world and keeps it going; and he tries to show that God exists by arguments of the form: since the world is of such-and-such a nature, there must be some being who made it and keeps it going; we give this being the name ' God '.

The name ' God ' thus introduced is regarded by Aquinas, not as a proper name, but as a general term (*nomen naturae*) so far as its mode of significance goes. There is indeed, he holds, only one God; but *there being many Gods* would be not an untrue supposition but merely unintelligible, if what were in question were the plurality of a given named individual. Aquinas rejects the idea that ' God ' is necessarily used equivocally by polytheists and by monotheists: he holds that the polytheist *may* be using the word ' God ' in the same sense when he says his idol is God, as the missionary when he says that the idol is not God but a senseless block. (In a work of Hindu propaganda I have seen it explained that by priestly consecration of an idol the Infinite becomes circumscribed, the Living One a lifeless block, the Omniscient insensible—such is the Divine condescension!) A strong point in favour of Aquinas's view is that ' God ' is *translated* into other languages, not *transliterated* as proper names are.

Though the word ' God ' is introduced to refer to the Maker and Sustainer of the world, that is not its definition. The term ' helium ' was first introduced to refer to an element that produced a certain line in the solar spectrum; but ' source of such-and-such a line in the solar spectrum' was not the definition of the term ' helium'; ' helium' was introduced as a new term in the category of ' nouns of material', like ' hydrogen' and ' gold', to refer to a material known only by inference not by examination of samples. Similarly, ' God' refers to the type of life that would belong to the Maker and Sustainer of the world, rather than to the acts of making and sustaining the world; and so, when the spiritual writers say that man may by grace ' become God', they mean that man may come to share in the special type of life that belongs to God, not that he may come to share in God's creative and sustaining activity.

These remarks on what mode of signification the term ' God' has do not make it the less true that to *prove* there is a God would be to *prove* that somebody made everything else, in the relevant sense of the verb ' made'. But what is the relevant sense, and how can it be learned and taught? Aquinas would say we learned it by analogy with other senses of ' making'; there are various familiar senses of the word, with complex likenesses and differences between them, and we may show how the word is applied to God by bringing out the likenesses and differences between this use and the familiar uses. For example, in one respect the use of the word when applied to God is more like ' the minstrel made music' than ' the blacksmith made a shoe'; for the shoe is made out of pre-existing material, and, once made, goes on existing independently of the smith; whereas the minstrel did not make the music out of pre-existing sounds, and the music stops if he stops making it; and similarly God did not make the world out of anything pre-existing, and its continued existence depends upon his activity.

It might be objected that it would be impracticable to specify all the necessary modifications of the concept *making* at the outset; yet without this we do not know what we have proved in proving that somebody *made* the world. But Aquinas would hold that the modifications need not be specified at the outset, but will be brought out dialectically from the fact that what is said to be made is the world. For instance, the world cannot have been made out of pre-existing material; for that material would itself already have been *in* the world. Again, though there is no making without change in that which is made, the making of the world would have to be without change occurring in the Maker, and in this respect unlike all other examples of making; for a Maker who was undergoing change because of making things would just be one of that system of interrelated changing things which we call the world, and so *not* the Maker of the world.

Again, someone may say that when all the requisite modifications of the old senses of ' made ' have been carried out, we are left not with a new, theological sense of the word but with an empty word whose sense has evaporated. Such evaporation of sense is a real danger with transferred uses of words. But we clearly could not take seriously a general objection to transferred uses of words; nor can the present objection be used to bar theological discussion at the very outset—though perhaps it might turn out that someone who had let himself follow theological discussion up to a point, for the sake of argument, found himself in a position to say: Surely by this series of qualifications you have destroyed the sense of the word ' made ' altogether.

I have spoken of God as the Maker of *the world*. This notion, as we shall see, raises problems; some theologians would wish to avoid them by proving God's existence from the existence of some casually chosen thing, not from the existence of the world, and might argue that in spite of using the term ' world ' (*mundus*) Aquinas's real mind was like theirs on this point. I think they are wrong as to the feasibility of such a proof, and it is fairly easy to show that Aquinas would not have agreed with them. If we ask an ordinary causal question about a particular thing, the answer need not be ' God ': the cause of a man's existence, say, is that he was generated by his parents. ' But couldn't we ask the same question about them? ' Certainly: but the possibility of asking a new question in no way implies that the original question was not rightly answered. ' But if a man had parents and they had parents and so on back *ad infinitum*, wouldn't this regress be vicious? ' Not at all. If the meaning of the original answer ' John was generated by his parents ' depended on our ability to say who *their* parents were, then the supposition of a chain of ancestors going back *ad infinitum* would involve the absurdity that we could not understand the original answer without completing the whole infinite series of answers. But on the contrary the original answer is understandable without raising the question of grandparents.

Aquinas accordingly holds that God cannot be reached by saying that this sort of causal chain must end in him: the chain could be endless. He uses the simile of an immortal blacksmith who has been making horseshoes from all eternity, and has naturally worn out no end of hammers in the process: the making of the horseshoe now on the anvil depends only upon the smith as efficient cause and the hammer currently in use as instrument; and though no end of hammers have in fact been broken in the past, they have nothing to do with the case. Similarly, God uses parents to produce a new human being: since they are mortal, he does not use the same pair of parents each time; but as regards understanding the production of this human being here and now, we need not bring into account all the past and perished generations of men, and it is no matter whether they were a finite or infinite series.

Just as the blacksmith, the hammer, and the horseshoe are related in the same way each time, so God's action is involved, according to Aquinas, in the same way for the production of each new generation of men, and each set of parents are alike ' second causes ' used instrumentally by the First Cause. The view that the backward series of generations logically has to be finite and terminate in God would on the contrary involve that in generating the first set of parents were causally closer to God than any subsequent parents: a strange result, which would surely be unwelcome to some proponents of the view.

It seems clear, then, that in spite of what a hasty reading of Aquinas's ' Five Ways ' might suggest, he did not think God could be reached by following to its end a causal chain starting from a random object. I shall argue that what is in fact essential to the ' Five Ways ' is something tantamount to treating the world as a great big object. (It is after all natural to us so to regard the world—' Heaven and Earth ', as it is called in the Old Testament—as the upper limit of the series: Earth, solar system, galaxy, cluster of galaxies, . . .) If the world is an object, it again seems natural to ask about it the sort of causal questions which would be legitimate about its parts. If it began to exist, what brought it into existence? In any case, what keeps it from perishing, as some of its parts perish? And what keeps its processes going? And to what end?

The question now arises whether there is any relevant difference if we are considering the world as a whole. Now of course someone might argue, in the style of Kant's antinomies, that we get into intractable problems if we use ' the world ' as a subject of predicates

—e.g. as to the world's being spatially or temporally finite or infinite. Aquinas was not unaware of such problems, but did not think them intractable: he thought e.g. that the world might or might not have had an infinite past duration, and that neither alternative led to contradiction. What would have appeared to him not worth discussion at all is the idea that, though we can speak without contradiction of the world as a whole, we cannot raise concerning it the sort of causal questions that we can raise concerning its parts. Why should we not raise them? It would be childish to say the world is too big for such questions to be reasonable; and to say the world is all-inclusive would be to beg the question—God would not be included in the world.

Further, Aquinas would not be embarrassed by the question: If it is reasonable to ask who made the world, then why is it not reasonable to ask who made God? For the world shares with its parts certain attributes that give rise to causal questions: it is a complex whole of parts and is in process of change. But, Aquinas would say, God is not a whole of parts and is unchangeable; so the same causal questions need not arise about him. Moreover, precisely because we should soon find ourselves in difficulties if we raised questions about the whole consisting of the world *plus* God—e.g. whether it is caused or uncaused, changeable or unchangeable—Aquinas would deny the legitimacy of speaking of such a whole.

If we now consider the ' five ways ' in detail, we shall see that four of them quite clearly depend on the legitimacy of that lumping-together of things by which one would pass from particular things to the world as a whole. The first two ' ways ' differ only in that one relates to processes of change and the other to things' coming to be; the further argument is quite parallel in each case. If B is the cause of a process going on in A, or of A's coming to be, then it may be that this happens because of a process in B that is caused by a further thing C; and C in turn may act because of a process in C caused by D; and so on. But now let us lump together the chain of things B, C, D, . . . , and call it X. We may predicate of each one of the causes B, C, D, . . . , *and also* of X as a whole, that it causes a process in A (or the coming-to-be of A) in virtue of being *itself* in process of change. But what is it that maintains this process of change in X? Something that cannot itself be in process of change: for if it were, it would just be one of the things in process of change that causes the process in A (or the coming-to-be of A); i.e. it would after all be just part of the changeable system of causes we called X, and not the cause of the process in X. Thus we are led to a changeless cause of the change and coming-to-be in the world: following Aristotle, Aquinas finds an adumbration of this is Anaxagoras, whose *Nous* was pervasive of the world without being mixed up with its materials or changed by its changes and on that very account had control over the world. The number of terms in X is irrelevant; and the changeless cause is introduced as the cause of the change in the whole system X, not as the last link in a chain, directly related only to the last link but one.

The third 'way' deals with contingent and necessary existence (Aquinas's actual word is '*possibilia*', not '*contingentia*'; but this does not signify). To understand this proof properly, we must first of all see the total mistake of trying here to construe contingency and necessity *à la* Leibniz, in terms of its being contingently or necessarily true that there is a so-and-so. This is a double misconstruction. First, 'there being' a so-and-so is not, as we saw, what Aquinas means by *esse*; and only this will turn out relevant to the proof. Secondly, the necessity or contingency that is here in question is not the *logical* necessity or contingency of some (existential) statement. Accordingly, the attacks on the notion of a logically necessary existential statement simply do not touch the third 'way' at all.

It may be objected that there is simply no sense to the word 'necessary', or none that can be coherently explained, apart from the logical necessity of statements. This thesis is upheld with great confidence in some recent essays on 'philosophical theology'; one author actually says concerning it: 'I have no space to demonstrate this here, and indeed I do not think that it is any longer in need of demonstration'. It may well be wondered how much study of modal logic—whether, indeed, any knowledge of there being such a discipline—lies at the bottom of such confidence. Anyhow, since what is 'necessary' is what 'cannot' not be, to say that 'necessary' can only refer to logical necessity is equivalent to saying that whatever cannot be so, *logically* cannot be so—e.g. that since I cannot speak Russian, my speaking Russian is logically impossible: which is absurd.

The true interpretation of the third 'way' may be seen e.g. from the parallel passage in the *Contra Gentes*; contingency of existence is established, not from I know not what 'sense' or 'experience' of contingency, but from the plain fact that some things are perishable; and again, the 'necessity' that is asserted of God is identified in Aristotelian style with eternity—with imperishable existence that has no liability to cease. With this clue, we may read the third 'way' as follows: Some things are genuinely liable to cease existing. But not every thing can be of this character: for then, Aquinas tacitly assumes, a universe entirely composed of perishable things would itself be perishable. (At this step there comes in the 'lumping together' previously discussed.) Now such a universe cannot have always existed; Aquinas finds it impossible that a universe with a genuine liability to perish, and without anything outside it to stop it perishing, should have existed an unlimited time without perishing. So, if such a universe is all that exists, then once upon a time nothing at all existed; but in that case nothing would exist now, which is absurd. 'Contingent', i.e. perishable, beings thus cannot exist alone: there must also be at least one 'necessary', i.e. imperishable, being. It is irrelevant to object to this proof that a material universe wholly composed of corruptible things might go on existing even if all its parts actually corrupted, because their matter could still exist under different forms; for the objection presupposes that this matter is not perishable as such, in the way that the things composed of it are; but then this matter will itself be one of the imperishable things Aquinas is talking about at this stage of the proof.

So far, then, what Aquinas claims to have shown is that the class of 'necessary' existents is not empty. He does not go on to argue that this class has only one member, namely God; nor did he believe this. Apart from the imperishable matter of things, spirits and human souls are 'necessary', in that they have no inherent liability to stop existing—*potentia ad non esse*; for they have no matter in their make-up that could assume a different form, or split up into many pieces, or (as people have sometimes fancied) be merged in a larger whole. What Aquinas does argue is that 'necessary', i.e. imperishable, things are imperishable either of themselves or derivatively; now there cannot be an endless series of things deriving imperishability each from its successor; therefore there must be a thing which not only is 'necessary' or imperishable, but is so underivatively or in its own right: and this is God. As regards the 'infinite series' part of this argument, he refers back to the second 'way'; accordingly, if I have rightly interpreted the second 'way', what is being argued there is as follows: A series of only-derivatively-imperishable things may be 'lumped together', and thus considered will form a system which is in its turn only-derivatively-imperishable; that, then, from which the system derives its imperishable character cannot form part of the system, and cannot occur in the series at any point, but rather each term of the series will owe its imperishable character to something outside the series.

The statement of the fourth 'way' in the *Summa Theologica* is odd and obscure to a modern reader; it involves *inter alia* an odd notion of degrees of truth—not *à la* Bradley, but apparently on the score that if one lie is a bigger lie than another, the truth opposed to one is a bigger truth than the truth opposed to the other. I can make no use of this idea, and will rather show how Aquinas might argue from the degrees of *esse* and of goodness, which also he here alludes to; I am not confident that this gives an historically correct exposition of the fourth 'way' (a proof which I sometimes suspect of being one of the indefensible remnants of Platonism in Aquinas's thought); but at least the argument I shall give can be paralleled in many parts of Aquinas's writings (e.g. in Ia q. 4 art. 2).

As we saw when we were deploying the arguments for a real distinction between a form and the corresponding *esse*, if any perfection occurs in a thing only to a degree, this requires a real distinction between the individual instance of the perfection and the degree to which that perfection is found. Now such occurrence of a perfection, Aquinas holds, requires a cause; for the fact that the perfection occurs gives no reason why it occurs only to such a degree and no more; so what accounts for the actual degree to which the perfection occurs—i.e., on Aquinas's view, accounts for the *esse* of that perfection—must be something outside the thing that has the perfection to that limited degree. The only source of perfections with regard to which such a problem would not again arise would have to be some thing possessing perfections not to a degree but without limit—God, who is 'infinite in all perfections' as the Penny Catechism says.

There is an apparent lacuna in this proof; the transition *from* a perfection's being derivative *to* its being derived from a being whose perfections are underivative has not been justified. But it would be easy to construct here an argument parallel to those used in the other three 'ways'. Alternatively, one might treat the fourth 'way', not as a new proof that there is a God, but as telling us something further about God—that the source of all process in the world, and of all beings in it, ' necessary ' or ' contingent ', is also the source of all perfections in the world, and possesses every perfection illimitably.

The fifth ' way ' uses that notion of ' tendencies ' which I have expounded. Aquinas argues that the process of the world as a whole (*omnia*) is goal-directed like the arrow shot by an archer, and must therefore owe its direction to the Cause of the world. Aquinas is not here appealing to empirical evidence of detailed ' adaptations '. His starting-point is the existence of a single cosmic order; and some such assumption is continually made in modern science, when (let us say) experiments in a terrestial laboratory and observations of an explosion in a distant nebula are treated as mutally relevant. Now causal order, on Aquinas's view, is describable only in terms of fulfilment of tendency; and if there is a Cause of the world, the cosmic tendencies will proceed from that Cause. Further Aquinas holds that, though a tendency need not be conscious, unconscious tendency is always derivative: unless the idea or consideration (*ratio*) of an end, and of an operation's being directed towards the end, is found in an agent, the agent's tendency towards the end, though it may be genuinely inherent in the agent and conformable to the agent's nature, will be a derivative tendency. So, Aquinas argues, the unconscious cosmic tendency is derivative, and presupposes an Agent outside the natural order who has thought and design.

Having thus established the existence of a God who is the cause of the world and of the processes in it, Aquinas discusses what we can say about God. We are at once arrested by his saying that as regards God we cannot answer the question ' *quid est?* ': if we cannot say what God is, what is the use of going on? This puzzle arises only from our forgetting the restricted sense of the Latin, as compared with the English, question. As I said, the word ' God ' refers to the type of life enjoyed by the Maker of the World; this is a type of life not to be found by observations *within* the world, like the life enjoyed by men or cats or cabbages, and this hiddenness of the life signified by the word ' God ' is expressed by Aquinas's denial that we know concerning God *quid est*. Aquinas is not saying that we cannot make true predications concerning God.

A problem now arises that would justifiably worry people with a

K

modern logical training: how are we to construe the various predications concerning God that Aquinas seeks to establish *before*, and as a
means to, establishing the proposition that there is only one God?
Since for Aquinas ' God ' is not a proper name but a general term, we
surely need to settle whether ' God is X ' means ' any God (any being
that is a God) is X ', or ' some God is X ', or ' the (one and only)
God is X '; we might suspect that Aquinas failed to specify this
because Latin so unfortunately lacks articles. But though Aquinas
omits to answer the question in advance, there is I think evidence
that he would have regarded such statements of natural theology as
not being of any of these types, but as being of the unquantifiable
type illustrated by ' man is an animal ' and ' man is a machine ':
the predicates (if truly predicated) attach to the subject in virtue of
the nature *being a God* that this term signifies. Once it has been
proved that there is only one God, any one of these statements may
be reconstrued as holding true of the one and only God.

A few remarks here on the logic of ' there is but one God ' and
' the one and only God '. On Russell's theory of descriptions, ' the
one and only God is X ' would be construed as meaning:

' For some y, y is God, and, for any z, if z is God, z is the same
as y, and y is X ';

and this, shorn of the final clause ' and y is X ', would also give the
analysis of ' there is but one God '. Aquinas would certainly have
objected, on general grounds, to the clause ' z is the same as y '; the
sameness, as we saw, must for him be specified by some general term
signifying a form or nature. Now the general term that we need to
supply here is clearly ' God '; so ' there is but one God ' will come
out as:

' For some y, y is God, and, for any z, if z is God, z is the same God
as y '.

It is important to notice that this would leave open the possibility
of there being several Divine Persons; there would still be but one
God, if we could truly say that any Divine Person was the same God
as any other Divine Person. Now different Persons' being the same
God is not manifestly impossible: for, in general, x and y may be
the same F although different things are true of x and of y. On the
other hand, since all the propositions of natural theology tell us only
what is true of a being in virtue of his being God, they cannot serve

to establish any distinction there might be between two Persons both of whom were God and the same God. Thus, so far as natural theology goes, the question whether many distinct Persons can be one and the same God is *demonstrably undecidable*, on Aquinas's view; this notion of something's being demonstrably undecidable within a given theory is one that recent logical research has made familiar and unexceptionable. As we shall see, Aquinas held there was a whole class of such questions. In this instance, he held it important not to prove God's unity in such a sense as to rule out the possibility of a Trinity; for certain ' monotheistic ' expressions are to be rejected as false by Christian believers—God is not to be spoken of as *sole, singular, unique,* or *solitary* (Ia q. 31 art. 3, 4).

When ' there is but one God ' is put into the misleading form ' God is One ', the numeral ' one ' is often taken to express an important Divine attribute—and curiously strong emotions are aroused, as is hinted by the initial capital. Aquinas wished to remove this august character from the word ' one '; the use of ' one ' in speaking about God (and of other numerals, e.g. ' three '—and ' five '—in Trinitarian theology) does not correspond to any Divine attribute whatsoever; nothing that is affirmatively predicable of God (*ponitur in divinis*) is expressed by a numerical term. ' One ' never in any case expresses an attribute of things, except when the word is taken in the ' discrete-quantity ' meaning of *being all in one piece,* which is not applicable to God; all that ' there is *one* God ' signifies over and above ' there is (a) God ' is *indivisio*—that it is *not* the case, for any x and y, that x is a *different* God from y.

Now how does Aquinas think this can be proved? There are two sorts of difference that there might be between two different animals in a zoo: material difference, between two individuals of the same kind, and formal difference, between individuals of different kinds. If a God is necessarily immaterial, then there cannot be material difference between two Gods; and Aquinas argues that a God must be immaterial, because God is the unchanging cause of change, whereas any body causes change only in that it simultaneously undergoes change (*nullum corpus movet non motum*). Just as Anaxagoras said that Mind must be ' unmixed ' with the material world in order to know and rule it, so Aquinas holds that the unchanging cause of all the changes in the physical world must itself be non-physical. Material multiplication of Gods is thus impossible. Further, the fourth ' way ' established that a God is infinite in all perfections; but if there were diverse Deities, one would excel in one perfection (say, justice) and another in another (say, mercy); so there cannot be a formal multiplication of Gods either, as the heathen have fancied. There remains indeed the possibility that two or more Persons, while equally unlimited in all perfections, should be distinct in virtue of some asymmetrical relation or relations holding between them. But any such Persons would be one and the same God; we must not be misled by a false imagination of the material difference that makes two human persons to be different men.

In the sequel, then, we may justifiably speak of proving the attributes of *God*; the question which God, or which Divine Person, we are talking about, will never arise.

Since God is immaterial, it follows at once on Aquinas's doctrine of thought that he is a living self-subsistent thought of himself. But God is not, as Aristotle allegedly believed, the only object of his own thought. If God is a self-subsistent thought, his causality of the world can only be that sort of causality in which what comes to be outside the agent is a fulfilment of a tendency proceeding from the agent's consideration; and this, as we saw, is Aquinas's account of *voluntary* causality. God, then, is the cause of the world in that he envisages such a world and and chooses that it should be. Here Aquinas' doctrine stands in noteworthy contrast with that of Spinoza, whose arguments are often paralleled in his most seriously considered objections.

Aquinas is insistent that God's creation of the world is absolutely free. He rejects the idea that God was bound to desire the best of all possible worlds; because there is no sense in talking of a best possible world, any more than of a biggest possible number. And still less can the creation of a world that is less good than another possible world be overwhelmingly attractive to the Divine Nature which already enjoys all perfections without measure—*ipsa suis pollens opibus, nil indiga nostri*. Moreover, God can be under no obligation to create anything: to whom could he owe it? In all God's works there is 'mercy' and ' justice': but the ' mercy ' whereby God gratuitously, without need or obligation, brings a creature into existence is more fundamental than the ' justice ' whereby he gives it what befits its nature.

We should notice that Aquinas's ascription of thought and will to God essentially derives from his account of the concepts *thought* and *will*. If these concepts were got from a particular experience, whether quasi-sensory or not, there would be no more ground for ascribing thought and will to God than for ascribing to him the passions we feel or even the colours we see. But Aquinas holds that a thought is in a way thought of just in virtue of one's having that thought, and needs no special added experience to bring it to the mind's ken; and that our reflection on the distinctive feature of thought shows this to be, not a recognisable quality like anger or redness, but a manner of *esse*, which accordingly there is nothing to hinder our ascribing to God even though we have no concrete knowledge of the Divine Life.

The false doctrine of will that we discussed under the heading *Operations and Tendencies* would lead to the supposition that the coming-to-be of the world was (at least logically) posterior to God's enacting within himself a ' volition ' or ' decree ' to create the world; many intractable problems have arisen about this supposed 'volition'. I have argued that, even as regards human voluntary actions, voluntariness consists for Aquinas in proceeding from the agent in a special manner, not in being the effect of something called a volition; certainly his proof that the world proceeds from God's will introduces no such intermediary entity as a creative ' volition ', but simply argues that God's mode of causality must be voluntary causality and not natural causality.

No question as to what God does in fact will to exist is soluble by natural theology; where free choice exists, no logic will enable us to deduce what is in fact chosen. (If, for instance, as Aquinas thought, a world with a beginning in time and one without a beginning are alike logically possible, natural theology cannot tell us which sort of world ours is.) There are thus an enormous number of questions that natural theology cannot answer; and no place for the presumptuous dream of Socrates in the *Phaedo,* that we could deduce what the world is like from our fancies of how it ought to be.

Before going further, we must expound Aquinas's doctrine of the Divine ' simplicity '.

It is part of the religious tradition to which Aquinas belongs to use abstract terms as well as concrete ones in designating God: to say that he is Wisdom, Power, and Love, not only wise, powerful and loving. One way of explaining this might be to say in Hobbes's style that the word we use for God ' ought to signify our desire to honour him with the best appellations we can think on ', and that these abstract words are mere ' attributes of honour '; and this would be supported by the interesting fact that just such abstract expressions do express special honour or devotion among men—a lover praises his mistress by saying ' you are sweetness itself ' rather than ' you are sweet ', and an ecclesiastic is addressed more ceremoniously as ' your Paternity ' than as ' Father '. One Praepositivus is mentioned by Aquinas as favouring this sort of account.

The generality of theologians, however, held that this use of abstract terms concerning God was not a mere honorific way of speaking, but must be taken seriously as expressing a real difference between God and creatures. Aquinas's doctrine concerning *quod* and *quo*, which I expounded in connexion with forms, is powerfully applied here: what is meant by ' God is Wisdom ', he holds, is that the terms ' God ' and ' the wisdom of God ' are both ways of referring to one and the same reality; and likewise ' the power of God ' again refers to the same reality. The attributes referred to by ' the wisdom of— ' and ' the power of — ' are indeed different, but the wisdom of God and the power of God are identical (cf. Ia q. 32 art. 3 ad 3 um).

The difficulty here is to exclude from one's mind the Platonism that Aquinas combats—the ' barbarous ' misconstruction of ' the wisdom of God ' as ' wisdom, which belongs to, is a property of, God'; if we do think on these lines, Aquinas will appear to be saying that wisdom and power are different, but God possesses both, and in him they are not different but identical—which is sheer self-contradiction. The analogy of mathematical functions, which I used before, proves valuable here too. 'The square of —' and 'the double of —' signify two quite different functions, but for the argument 2 these two functions both take the number 4 as their value. Similarly, ' the wisdom of — ' and ' the power of — ' signify different forms, but the individualizations of these forms in God's case are not distinct from one another; nor is either distinct from God, just as the number 1 is in no way distinct from its own square. And again, ' the *esse* of God ', ' that by which God *is* ', signifies nothing distinct from Him-who-is.

It is a very short way from these considerations to the severe difficulties of the view that discourse concerning God is ' analogical '. It would be better to say that it turns out to be analogical: what happens, on Aquinas's view, is that we first call God ' wise '; then discover that ' the wisdom of God ' is a designation of God himself, whereas the like does not hold of any other being whom we rightly call ' wise '; and thus reflecting upon this, we see that ' wise ' cannot be applied to God in the same way as to other beings. The difficulty is to show that this conclusion is not a mere *reductio ad absurdum:* starting from the premise that God can be called 'wise', we reach the conclusion that he cannot in the ordinary sense be so called, which surely contradicts the premise.

An attempt has been made to remove the difficulty by appealing to ' proportionality ': God's wisdom, to be sure, is entirely different from man's, but God's wisdom is to God as man's wisdom is to man. This is, of course, a mathematical metaphor—' x is to a as b is to c; required to find x '—and it is a thoroughly bad one. A rule-of-three sum can be worked only if three of the quantities involved are known; but God is not ' known ' in the relevant sense— i.e. something encountered as an item in the world. (As I explained in discussing *esse*, knowing *that there is* a God is a very different matter.) Moreover, since God's wisdom is supposedly identical with God, but not man's wisdom with man, the metaphor breaks down at once: for we cannot have in mathematics that x is to a as b is to c, and $x = a$, but not $b = c$.

Our own mathematical metaphor of functions does something to lessen these difficulties. We can produce an actual example of a number that is its own square and its own cube, namely the number 1; but there may very well be functions, say F ( ) and G ( ), such that we can prove the mathematical theorem that, for some x or other, $x = F(x) = G(x)$, without being able to cite a particular number satisfying this equation; we may even be able to prove that any number which did satisfy the equation would be too large to be distinctly apprehended. And this is like what Aquinas is maintaining about God: that we can know which attributes are meant by general terms like ' wise ' and ' just ', and also *know that* there is a being, whom we call ' God ', whose wisdom and justice and *esse* are identical with him and with one another; even though we *have no insight into* the simple nature that verifies all these predicates simultaneously, without room for a distinction between *quod* and *quo*, between the individual occurrence of attributes and the God in whom they occur, or between God and his *esse*.

There is, then, no obvious incoherence in the doctrine that God is his own Nature, his own attributes, his own *esse*. But how is this doctrine proved? and what are its consequences?

The fourth ' way ' as I interpret it (an interpretation certainly conformable to what Aquinas says elsewhere) is in essentials the argument that what possesses a perfection only to a degree does not possess it underivatively. God's perfections are illimitable because there is in no case a distinction between the perfection he has and the degree to which he has it, as there would be if it were possible for him to have that very perfection to a higher degree; and where such a distinction does exist, a perfection is necessarily derivative. Now for Aquinas the degree to which a perfection is possessed must be regarded as the *esse* of that instance of the perfection. We may thus naturally pass to a generalised form of the argument. If there is ever a distinction between an individualised form or nature and the corresponding *esse*, then the *esse* of that form or nature must be caused; an individualised form or nature that is not its own *esse* cannot have *esse* in its own right. God, then, must be his own *esse*; otherwise there would be a cause that supplied *esse* to the Divine Nature, which is absurd. And each Divine perfection is identical with its own *esse*, and thus with God.

From this doctrine of God's ' simplicity ', it follows that God is unchangeable and eternal. Of any changeable thing x, we have to say that it remains the same F while changing from G to not-G or *vice versa*; but if God changed from being G to being not-G or *vice versa* while remaining the same God, we should have to assert a real distinction between his G-ness and his possession of the Divine Nature, which we cannot do. So God is in every respect unchangeable. Eternity is defined by Aquinas (following Boethius) as the simultaneous and complete possession of unending life; being unchangeable, God is eternal.

We must not conceive of God's eternity as like the timelessness of mathematics: the primeness of the number 7 simply has no relation to dates, whereas God's eternity is compresent with every part of time; so we can properly say ' God existed yesterday ', ' God sees to-day what men do ', whereas ' 7 was prime yesterday ' is non-sensical. Aquinas even holds that different predicates are true of God at different times; if Socrates first sits down and then gets up, then we must say of God first that he knows that Socrates is sitting and then that he knows that Socrates is standing. How this is possible without a change within God's mind Aquinas does not try to say; the way an eternal mind operates is naturally not fully understandable by us. (Ia q. 14 art. 15 ad 3 um.)

Let us then sum up Aquinas's teaching as to man's natural knowledge of God. In an inchoate form, this knowledge is available to all men who are sufficiently reflective to think of the world-order as a whole and wonder how it came to be and how it is sustained; and most men have believed in its governance by superior power to which they gave the name God. But just as men who can tell living from non-living things may give the most grotesque account of what it is to have life or soul (e.g. that the soul is a small or rarefied man), so men who recognise that there is a God ruling the world may give grotesque accounts of him (e.g. that he is an immortal and powerful man). There is no innate idea of God by appeal to which such follies are refutable.

Natural theology can show us some of the main attributes of God, and expose some of the grosser errors about him. But a serious study of natural theology requires a rigorous philosophical training, for which few have leisure, talents, or inclination. Moreover, the divergent views of great philosophers who have pursued this study show that there is still risk of grave error.

What is more, the God of whom natural theology apprises us is frightening: we depend for our very existence from moment to moment on a Being of infinite knowledge and power, whose will in our regard we know in advance to be beyond our skills of calculation. It is just as well that we should be frightened: the fear of the Lord is the beginning of wisdom. But if wisdom were not more than this, we might well despair, thinking of man as he is; what if God should will that this miserably wicked race should utterly destroy itself?

For Aquinas, however, the wisdom of natural theology is only the beginning: our puzzles are replaced by certainties, and our fear by hope, because of the relevation God has freely given through Jesus Christ.

> Sinners be glad, and penance do,
>   And thank your Maker heartfully;
> For he that ye might not come to
>   To you is comen full humbly
>   Your soulis with his blood to buy
> And loose you of the fiend's arrest,
>   And only of his own mercy;
> *Pro nobis Puer natus est.*

FREGE

Friedrich Ludwig Gottlob Frege was born at Wismar on November 8th, 1848. His father was principal of a girls' high school; his mother's maiden name (Bialloblotzky) suggests Polish extraction. He was a student at Jena for two years (1869-71) and thereafter for five terms at Göttingen; he studied mathematics, physics, chemistry, and philosophy. He took his Doctorate of Philosophy at Göttingen in 1873. He became a Privatdozent at Jena in 1874, an ausserordentlicher Professor in 1879, and an ordentlicher Professor in 1896. He retired in 1914, and died in July 1925.

Frege's work was almost wholly unappreciated during his lifetime; he rightly considered his colleagues at Jena incompetent to understand him, and said this in print, which cannot have made his relations with them happy. The choice of one Schubert to write an encyclopaedia article on Numbers provoked Frege into publishing a vitriolic tract on Schubert's unfitness for the task. He had, however, the comfort of contacts with Russell and Wittgenstein, who both retained a deep impression of his genius.

Wittgenstein's story of his relations with Frege was as follows. ' I wrote to Frege, putting forward some objections to his theories, and waited anxiously for a reply. To my great pleasure, Frege wrote and asked me to come and see him.

' When I arrived I saw a row of boys' school caps and heard a noise of boys playing in the garden. Frege, I learned later, had had a sad married life—his children had died young, and then his wife; he had an adopted son, to whom I believe he was a kind and good father.

' I was shown into Frege's study. Frege was a small, neat man with a pointed beard, who bounced around the room as he talked. He absolutely wiped the floor with me, and I felt very depressed; but at the end he said "You must come again", so I cheered up.

' I had several discussions with him after that. Frege would never talk about anything but logic and mathematics; if I started on some other subject, he would say something polite and then plunge back into logic and mathematics. He once showed me an obituary on a colleague, who, it was said, never used a word without knowing what it meant; he expressed astonishment that a man should be praised for this!

' The last time I saw Frege, as we were waiting at the station for my train, I said to him "Don't you ever find any difficulty in your theory that numbers are objects?" He replied " Sometimes I seem to see a difficulty—but then again I don't see it ".'

ONE of the main goals Frege set before himself in his intellectual career was to devise an adequate and perspicuous symbolism to express mathematical propositions and deductions. It might perhaps be supposed that the ordinary symbolism of mathematics was already pretty well adequate; but Frege, for sufficient reasons, did not think so; ' in actual fact there are perhaps no scientific works where you will find more wrong expressions, and consequently wrong thoughts, than in mathematical ones '.

Two simple examples will show what sort of ' wrong expressions ' Frege objected to. (1) ' $\sqrt{4} = \pm 2$ ' pretends to say what *the* square root of 4 is equal to, but since 4 has two square roots there is no such thing as *the* square root of 4; and again, ' ± 2 ' looks like the sign of a definite number, but there is no such number as plus-or-minus 2. (2) In elementary algebra division by 0 is forbidden as ' meaningless ', because it leads to wrong consequences; but it is practically impossible to devise prohibitory rules to exclude this ' meaningless ' operation; for one would need to exclude disguises for zero from being denominators, as well as the figure ' 0 ' itself, and e.g. ' x—y ' may be such a disguise (as in a sophistical proof, well known to schoolboys, that $2 = 1$), but you cannot say that the use of ' x—y ' as a denominator is ' meaningless '.

The symbolisms Frege found in use by the logisticians of his time also appeared to him gravely defective. By an achievement of great genius, he managed to overcome all the difficulties. Although difficult to print, Frege's symbolism is extremely perspicuous—one can see at a glance how a proposition is articulated and how an inference is performed; and it is a logically adequate symbolism, which could be extended, according to strictly formulated rules of definition, to perform any required task in mathematical logic.

In this compass I cannot devote any space to systematic elucidation of Frege's symbolism; but it had to be mentioned at the outset because it was the effort of devising it that obliged Frege to formulate his revolutionary views about the philosophy of logic. As has been said, a good symbolism is like a teacher. It is indeed quite possible that a philosophy of logic primarily aiming at a satisfactory account of mathematical thought may be inadequate in its account of non-mathematical thought; but if a philosopher is not willing to be taught by the requirements of mathematics at all, we cannot expect his philosophy of logic to be worth much.

In the preface to his youthful work, *Begriffsschrift*, Frege states that he found it was no use to try and fit in the ordinary distinction of subject and predicate into his symbolism. I think this remark offers us a useful clue to his thought. If we start from the sort of account of subject and predicate that was given by the ' traditional ' logicians (like Ueberweg, or Joseph in England), and then consider Frege's way of eliminating the various mistakes and confusions it contains, we shall find that we have described some of the main lines of Frege's thought.

Traditionally, the important sort of proposition is a proposition ' with one subject and one predicate ', and the important sort of inference is a syllogism with premises of this sort; hypothetical and disjunctive propositions and reasonings are admitted into logic on sufferance, as a sort of appendix. The predicate is what is asserted or denied of the subject. The same ' term ' that appears as a predicate in one proposition may be the subject of another proposition.

The first thing to make clear is the distinction between sign and thing signified. The man Socrates is obviously different from the name ' Socrates ', but in speaking of the subject of a proposition about Socrates, people would often vacillate as to whether the man or the name was the subject. I shall adopt the convention that ' Socrates ', not the man Socrates, is the subject of ' Socrates is wise '; and similarly, that ' wise ', not what it signifies, is the predicate in this proposition. I shall however say that the predicate is *predicated of* Socrates, not of his name; and on the other hand that it is *attached to* the name, not the man. I shall use *double* quotes, henceforth, when I wish to speak *about* the quoted expression. The need for care in distinguishing ' use and mention ', a commonplace of modern logic, was borne in upon Frege in the course of controversies; he uses quotes carelessly and informally in his youthful works, but quite strictly in *Grundgesetze*. A certain ' formalist ' mathematician, who professed to hold that numbers were just numeral marks with which we played a ' game ', nevertheless spoke of a series of continually diminishing ' numbers '; Frege affected to think he meant a series of *figures* printed in progressively smaller founts of type, and silenced his indignant protests by saying that this was how 'formalists' always ran away from the consequences of taking their theories seriously.

A more serious confusion is wrapped up in the expression " asserted in regard to a subject ", by which predicates are traditionally described. A predicate may obviously be attached to a subject in a clause that does not serve to make any assertion—e.g. the antecedent or consequent of a hypothetical, or a clause of an alternative proposition; and this in no way alters the sense of the predicate. Even when a subject-predicate proposition does stand by itself and serve to make an assertion, the assertoric force attaches to the proposition as a whole, not specially to the predicate. The traditional notion of a predicate thus fuses together elements that logically have no genuine connexion.

Frege introduced the assertion sign " ⊢ " to flag asserted propositions. The use of this sign clears up a number of obstinate problems. (i) Does "p" mean the same both times in "m, if m then p, *ergo* p ", or again in " not m, m or p, ergo p "? If it does, there is no inference, for the assertion " p " is already part of the premises; if it does not, the inference is vitiated by the ambiguity of " p ".—Frege could write such inferences as follows: " ⊢m, ⊢(if m then p), *ergo* ⊢p "; " ⊢(not m), ⊢(m or p), *ergo* ⊢p ". The content asserted in " ⊢p " occurs also in the premise " ⊢ (if m then p) " or " ⊢(m or p) ", but it is not asserted in this latter context. (ii) How can one validly perform a *reductio ad absurdum*—a reasoning of the form " Supposing that p, it follows that not p; so not p "? It looks like a self-destructive procedure—like trying to build a house by removing the foundations to build the upper floors.—Frege could reply that " Supposing that p, it follows that not p " is not to be symbolized as " ⊢p, *ergo* ⊢ (not p) " (which would certainly be absurd and self-destructive) but as " ⊢ (if p, then not p) ", from which one may infer "⊢(not p) " without any retracing of an admittedly false step.

In his earliest work, *Begriffsschrift*, Frege had not quite fought his way out of the old confusion between predication and assertion, and wrote as if his introduction of the assertion-sign were a reduction of all predicates to the single predicate " is the case " or " is true ". The notion of predicate here employed is the old incoherent notion of a predicate as including assertion; and even if this notion were not incoherent, the reduction of the class of such predicates to one single number could have only technical, not philosophical, interest.

L

But in his later work *Ueber Sinn und Bedeutung* Frege shows why this account of the assertion-sign will not do: a proposition of the form " the thought that . . . is true ", like any other proposition, has the same content whether it is being asserted or not; " is true ", like any other predicate, is part of an assertable content, but has no assertoric force. The assertion-sign is not a predicate; it is *sui generis*.

Another mistake in the traditional view was to rank assertion and negation together as polar opposites and thus as logically on a par. Frege exposed this mistake in the same way as the confusion between predication and assertion—by drawing attention to the occurrence of " not ", or of predicates, in unasserted clauses within assertions. " If p, then q; p; *ergo* q " and " If not m, then q; not m; *ergo* q " are plainly arguments of the same form; this makes it apparent that the asserted premise " not m " should not be symbolized say as " ⊣m ", as though we did something to the content of " m " that was the reverse of assertion (" ⊣ "), but rather as " ⊢ (not m) ". Negation is part of the content of a proposition, whether that proposition is asserted or not.

There is an apparent inconsistency in Frege's attitude to the question whether negation attaches to a proposition as a whole or rather (as traditional logicians sometimes held) to the predicate. We find him saying *both* that e.g. " that man is uncelebrated " denies the thought expressed in " that man is celebrated "—we are not to think that just one word has its content negated—*and* that the predicate in " all mammals are land-dwellers " is really not " are land-dwellers " but rather " all . . . are land-dwellers ", because we obtain a contradictory statement by negating the predicate of the one we started with, and here what we have to negate is not " are land-dwellers " (to " are not land-dwellers ") but " all . . . are land-dwellers " (to " not all . . . are land-dwellers ").—A reconciliation of these views is, however, possible: for Frege, negation primarily attaches to statements as wholes, and what is meant by one predicate's being the negation of another has to be explained in terms of this—it means that the two predicates yield a pair of contradictory statements if we attach them to any one out of a certain range of subjects. Thus, " is a land-dweller" and "is not a land-dweller" are one another's negations in regard to any singular term as subject; and so are " all . . . are land-dwellers " and "not all . . . are land-dwellers ", in regard to any general term insertable in the blanks.

In traditional logic there was some vacillation as to whether in a phrase like " is not wise " or " are not wise " the negation belongs with the copula or with the general term following it. For Frege no such question even arose; he was convinced that the copula (when followed by a general term) is an accidental grammatical feature of language, with no special content whatsoever. Accordingly, for him it is all one whether we take the predicate in " Socrates is (not) wise " to be " is (not) wise " or just " (not) wise ". With this there went a rejection of the view that there are logically different sorts of copula—e.g. the copulas of class-inclusion and class-membership: ' If instead of " all mammals are vertebrates " we say " the class of mammals is included in the class of vertebrates ", the predicate is not " the class of vertebrates " but " included in the class of vertebrates '; and " is included " is not the copula alone but the copula *plus* a bit of the predicate '.

This does not mean that Frege was indifferent to the distinction that his contemporaries were trying to make by speaking of class-membership and class-inclusion copulas; it was one that he constantly emphasized, only he drew it in a different way. (Medieval logic had sharply distinguished between singular and universal propositions, regarding " every Plato is a philosopher " not as a legitimate way of writing " Plato is a philosopher " but as positively ill-formed, *impropria, incongrua*; the rubbing out of this distinction was one of the great faults of the ' traditional ' logic.) Frege's account of the distinction had nothing to do with the copula; for him, the difference between " Socrates is a Greek " and " every philosopher is a Greek " lies, first, in the difference between a proper name (" Socrates ") and a general term—in his language a ' concept-word '—like " philosopher "; secondly, as we saw, in that the logical predicate of the second sentence is not " is a Greek " but " every . . . is a Greek ". " Is " means the same (viz nothing at all) in both sentences. If we take what Frege called ' a mechanical or quantitative view ' of the matter, and regard " Greek " as standing for the class of Greeks and " every philosopher " as standing for the whole class of philosophers, then indeed we are driven to interpret " is " as signifying a relation of class-membership in " Socrates is a Greek " and one of class-inclusion in " every philosopher is a Greek ". But Frege would regard such a view as little better than the traditional confusion; it seemed to him radically wrong to treat "every philosopher" as a logical subject at all.

Some slight use of Scholastic terms in Frege's works makes it possible that he actually recognised the medieval distinction between *nomen individui* and *nomen naturae* to be much the same as his own distinction between a proper name and a concept-word. If we confine the term " proper name " to logically simple designations of single objects—a description satisfied by what are ordinarily called proper names—then the resemblance between the medieval and the Fregean distinction becomes strikingly close. If we interpret "A" as a concept-word, a *nomen naturae*, then " is there more than one A? " is certainly an intelligible question, even if the right answer to it is obviously, or even by logical necessity, negative; but if we take "A" as the proper name of an individual, no such question is co-herently framable, for the plurality (there being more than one) of a given individual is merely unintelligible. The last sentence expresses a view that would have been accepted as true both by Frege and e.g. by Aquinas; they both explain away in similar style such apparent attributive uses of proper names as " Trieste is no Vienna " or " he is an Achilles " ; and they both use the possibility of asking " Is there more than one—? " as a test for distinguishing the different senses of a word like " sun " or " moon ", which is sometimes a descriptive term with a significant plural (" the suns in the Milky Way ", " the moons of Jupiter ") and sometimes a proper name whose plural would be nonsense.

In calling a numeral sign like " seven " or " 7 " a proper name, Frege is not stretching the *notion* of a proper name; the term will appear justified or not according as one accepts or does not accept his view of numbers as objects. Frege, however, applied the term "proper name " far more widely than to simple signs for single objects; he applied it also to complex designations of objects—to what are commonly called definite descriptions. This extension of the term appears, on his own premises, very much open to exception. If we take "A" to represent a concept-word or a many-worded concept-expression, then it is arguable that " (is) *the* A" will likewise be a concept-expression; " x is *the* A" will mean " x is *an* A and nothing besides x is *an* A". To be sure, it is logically impossible for more than one thing to be *the* A; but Frege himself insists that we must sharply distinguish between a proper name and a concept-word that can apply only to one thing.

On the view here being argued against Frege, there is no more a

special copula of identity (as he thought there was) in " is the A "
than there is a copula of class-membership or class-inclusion (as he
thought there was not) in " is an A "; in all these contexts " is " has
no special content of its own at all. When I say " nobody is *the*
King of Switzerland " or " no number is *the* square root of 4 ", I am
not trying to designate a person or a number, and then saying that
nobody is identical with that person or no number equal to that
number; I am, in Fregean language, specifying a concept that could
apply to at most one person or number, and saying that in fact nothing
answers to this concept.

It is fairly easy to see why Frege wished to class complex singular
designations together with logically simple singular terms like ordinary proper names. One reason was his adoption of the view that an
ordinary proper name is just an abbreviation for a definite description: e.g. that "Aristotle " is short for something like " the pupil of
Plato who taught Alexander the Great ". This view has some slight
plausibility for names of historical characters, but none at all as regards
names of one's own acquaintances. Frege's reasons for adopting the
disguised-description theory of proper names cannot have been, as
Russell's reasons were, epistemological; for it is certain that he wholly
rejected an epistemological approach to philosophical problems. (His
lifelong attitude was: First settle what is known, and how these
known truths are to be analysed and articulated—and only then can
you profitably begin to discuss what makes these truths dawn upon a
human being; if you try to *start* with a theory of knowledge, you
will get nowhere.) I do not know how his adoption of the disguised-
description theory is to be explained.

Frege rightly emphasizes the total difference between statements
of the form " there is no such thing as — " when the blank is filled
with a concept-expression and when it is filled with a proper name.
In the latter case we are alluding to, and deprecating, a certain use
of a proper name. There is no such thing as Cerberus: i.e. don't be
frightened by those stories—I was only making believe to use " Cerberus " as the name of a dog, not really making statements about a
dog so named. There is no such thing as Vulcan: i.e. the astronomer
who thought he had identified a new planet, and christened it
" Vulcan ", was mistaken. The upshot of the remark is to exclude a
certain use of " Cerberus " or " Vulcan " as the subject of statements
seriously intended. On the other hand, " there is no such thing as an

intra-Mercurian planet " is in no way meant to exclude the use of the concept-expression " intra-Mercurian planet " in serious astronomical statements; on the contrary, it is itself an instance of a serious astronomical statement in which that concept-expression is used. ' Proper names without any reference are illegitimate in science; empty concepts cannot be banished.'

This very difference, however, really tells against Frege's notion of the complex proper name. " There is no such person as King Grognio " serves to exclude use of the proper name " King Grognio " from serious political discourse; " there is no such person as the King of Switzerland " is on the contrary a piece of serious political discourse in which the vacuous description " the King of Switzerland " is used. By this criterion, a definite description would not be a proper name but a concept-expression.

It is thus arguable that, even on his own premises, Frege ought not to have assimilated definite descriptions to proper names; but he did do so, and extended the use of the term " proper name " accordingly. This was certainly not due, as some critics of Frege have asserted, to a general preconception that every kind of expression must stand for some object, or else for some ' queer ' non-object. Meinong had such a preconception, and so had Russell when he wrote *The Principles of Mathematics*; Frege never had. As we have seen, Frege thought it foolish to take " every man " as standing for every man, or for the class of men either. Again, unlike Russell, Frege rejected the view that the letters used as variables in mathematics stand for variable numbers. Again, though often accused of assimilating statements to names, Frege expressly denies that either a sentence when used to make a statement—one that would in his notation have the assertion-sign prefixed—, or the assertion-sign itself, stands for anything at all. In *Function und Begriff* he says: ' " $\vdash 2 +3=5$ " does not designate anything; it asserts something.' (The assertion-sign cannot even form *part* of a designation of an object.) We ought, therefore, to take seriously Frege's view that a given sort of expression regularly does stand for something or other; we cannot just write it off, as what he would anyhow say about any sort of expression.

There is a stronger reason for Frege's view of the complex designation than those which we have so far discussed; and it probably had more influence on Frege himself. It relates to a very familiar fact—freedom of substitution between simple and complex designations of numbers in mathematics. The working mathematician may feel no difficulty over substituting for one another a simple and a complex designation of a given number, e.g. "e" and "the limit of $(1+1/n$ to the nth power) as n increases indefinitely". But the difficulty is there, even if it is not felt. We are not justified in using "e" as a simple sign for the number that is the limit of $(1+1/n$ to the nth power) as n increases indefinitely, unless we know that some number does answer to this description; and unlike Ramanujan most of us cannot decide such questions off hand—e.g. we cannot see on inspection that there is a limit of $(1+1/n$ to the nth powers), but *not* of (the sum of the reciprocals of the numbers 1 to n), as n increases indefinitely. Of these two, equally well-formed, descriptions, one has a definite number answering to it, the other has not: thus we may not without more ado replace a well-formed description by a simple numerical sign. And Frege would say it was a defect in ordinary mathematical symbolism to allow of complex designations' being formed without numbers answering to them; he would advocate an artificial reconstruing of mathematical symbolism to avoid this. E.g. the symbol now read as "the limit of F(n) as n increases indefinitely" could be reinterpreted thus: if there is a number x that is the limit of F (n) as n increases indefinitely, the symbol is to stand for x; if there is no such number, it is to stand for zero.

But, it may be objected, the ordinary way of reading mathematical symbolism gives no clear support for assimilating complex designations to simple ones; and is Frege's reformed way of reading called for unless that assimilation has already been justified? (It would in that case certainly be called for; ' proper names without any reference are illegitimate in science' , and if empty complex designations were to be assimilated to empty proper names, they too would be illegitiate.) The question thus becomes: supposing we reject the assimilation, is there any alternative view of the complex designation, on Fregean premises?

Here we need to notice a difference between two ways of using a definite or indefinite description " D "—a directly predicative use, i.e. in a context of the form " so-and-so is (not) D ", and a ' referential ' use, i.e. in a context where a proper name could equally well stand instead of " D ". Illustrations of these uses would be

"Ahab isn't a dog (Johnson's dog) " and "Ahab fought a dog (Johnson's dog) " respectively. In the latter context the proper name " Fido " could stand instead of the description " a dog " or " Johnson's dog '. This is not true in the same way for the former context. Of course, so far as grammar goes, we have "Ahab isn't Fido " and "Ahab isn't a dog " apparently differing in just the same way as "Ahab fought Fido " and "Ahab fought a dog." But Frege rightly refuses to be led by grammar at this point. To use his sort of language; in "Ahab isn't a dog ", " a dog " stands for a concept, under which it is being denied that Ahab falls; but " Fido " certainly has no such role in "Ahab isn't Fido "—the force of this is that Ahab is *other than* Fido. Thus in "Ahab isn't Fido " we may *rightly* ascribe a special force to the copula, which it has not got in "Ahab isn't a dog "; and the two statements therefore do not differ *only* through the replacement of a description by a proper name.

But Frege would hold, so far as concerns indefinite descriptions, that the ' referential ' use is reducible to a predicative use: " Jemima fought a dog " is reducible to " it is true of something or other both that it is a dog and that Jemima fought it ". And there is as yet no apparent reason for not applying the same method of reduction to " Jemima fought Johnson's dog ". We have still found no good reason for the treatment of definite descriptions as complex proper names rather than as concept-expressions; for indefinite descriptions also admit of an apparently non-predicative or ' referential ' use, and Frege's device for explaining this away would also explain away the ' referential ' use of a definite description, reducing it to purely predicative occurrence of the same description.

This reduction, however, runs us into difficulties in mathematics. Let " F(D) " schematically represent a predicate " F( ) " (e.g. " — is prime ") attached to a complex numerical designation " D "; and let " p " schematically represent some proposition. How are we to eliminate the ' referential ' occurrence of the complex designation from " if F(D), then p "? Two ways of doing this appear equally justified:

(1) If it is true of some number x both that F (x) and that x is D, then p.

(2) It is true of some number x both that x is D and that, if F(x), then p.

And if we do not as yet know whether " D " is an empty designation, then for all we know (1) and (2) may actually differ as regards truth—if " D " is empty, (1) may be true and (2) false.

The trouble arises over how much of the proposition " if F(D), then p " we take to be the context in which " D " occurs—to be the ' scope ' of the description " D ", as Russell would say; in (1) the ' scope ' is taken to be just " F(D) "; in (2), the whole proposition " if F(D), then p ". Such troubles about ' scope ' arise only for descriptions, not for proper names. As regards indefinite descriptions, we can avoid all such trouble by simply never using them, in the symbolic language of mathematics, in the ' referential ' way; the method of avoiding their ' referential ' use will be made clearer when we discuss quantification. But there is no question of excluding from mathematics a ' referential ' use of complex singular designations—i.e. the facility of substituting them for simple designations (like " 7 " or " e ") of the same numbers.

At this point there becomes relevant Frege's way of reconstruing complex singular designations, so that there always is a number answering to each well-formed designation; in that case a statement of the form " if F(D), then p " would never be true on interpretation (1) and false on interpretation (2)—its truth-conditions would be definite and unambiguous, regardless of what we took as the ' scope ' of " D ".

Frege maintains that the sense of a proposition (so far as logic is concerned—as opposed e.g. to its aesthetic value) is fully determined by stating what necessary and sufficient truth-conditions it has. If we do state these truth-conditions we not only determine whether the proposition is true, but also fix its sense, which is the sense of: Such-and-such conditions are fulfilled.

This doctrine is to be found in some medieval logicians, pretty explicitly; and also, by direct derivation from Frege, in Wittgenstein's *Tractatus*. It is merely silly to be prejudiced for or against it by the fact that some other authors have held it in conjunction with a ' verificationist ' epistemology and an ontology of ' sense-data '; it has no logical connexion with such doctrines, however many people have thought it has.

On this view of sense, Frege's convention for definite descriptions makes the sense of propositions containing them, like that of propositions containing proper names, to be determinate regardless of

' scope '. And this does make it plausible, after all, to maintain that
if we follow Frege in so construing complex singular designations
that they are never vacuous, then we may also regard them, when so
construed, as essentially similar in logic to proper names.

Frege's convention for definite descriptions is a perfectly coherent
one, and will be employed in the rest of our discussions (unless
otherwise stated). Its divergence from ordinary usage in no way
counts against it. Much ink used to be spilt on whether logicians had
the right to construe "A or B " as covering "A and B ", but nobody
worries about that now; and nobody to speak of ever has worried
about whether Aristotle had the right to construe " some S is P " as
covering the case when every S is P. Frege's convention about
definite descriptions is of the same order as the logicians' accepted
streamlining of the use of " or " and " some ".

On the other hand, Frege was certainly wrong if he thought his
convention was the only logically coherent one; an alternative would
be the *Principia Mathematica* method of assigning a ' scope ' to
definite descriptions by strict rules (though these rules are not easy
to formulate exactly, and the *Principia* formulation is in fact faulty).
As Wittgenstein says in the *Tractatus*, what is again and again
philosophically significant is that a certain convention *can* be followed
in a satisfactory logical symbolism; there is no need to show that this
is the only possible convention.

To adopt Frege's convention about definite descriptions does not
commit us to his theory of them; but, as I said, the theory becomes
plausible when it is applied to sentences in which all definite descriptions are read in Frege's way; since we are adopting his convention,
we may accordingly take this theory for granted as a matter of exposition.

Let us, then, consider the way complex designations are constructed. The expressions

$$\text{`` } 2 \cdot 2^2 + 2 \text{ ''},$$
$$\text{`` } 2 \cdot 3^2 + 3 \text{ ''},$$
$$\text{`` } 2 \cdot 7^2 + 7 \text{ ''},$$

designate the numbers 10, 21, 105 respectively; they are derived in
a uniform way from designations of the respective numbers 2, 3, 7.
Mathematicians say that we have here a *function* whose *values* for the
respective *arguments* 2, 3, 7 are 10, 21, 105. Now Frege draws our

attention to the way that e.g. " $2 \cdot 7^2 + 7$ ", a designation of this function's value for the argument 7, is analysable into a sign for the argument, " 7 ", and a sign for the function. We clearly cannot, however, just remove the two occurrences of " 7 " from " $2 \cdot 7^2 + 7$ " and take what is left to be the sign of the function; for " $2 \cdot \ \ ^2 +$ " means nothing, and moreover contains no indication that the same numerical sign is to be supplied both as base of the index " 2 " and after the *plus* sign. The sign for the function is in fact not an identifiable printed shape like " 7 " or " $2 \cdot 7^2 + 7$ ".

Frege does to be sure speak of the function $2 \cdot \xi^2 + \xi$, and call " $2 \cdot \xi^2 + \xi$ " the name of a function; but of course " $2 \cdot \xi^2 + \xi$ " is not physically a part of " $2 \cdot 7^2 + 7$ ", as " 7 " is; so clearly " $2 \cdot \xi^2 + \xi$ " is not a symbol for a function in the same way as " 7 " and " $2 \cdot 7^2 + 7$ " are symbols of numbers. This must indeed have been clear to Frege himself; for in using the letter " ξ " he mentions that he chose this letter just *because* it is never used in any well-formed formula of his system. This letter is for him no essential part of the functional sign, but is a mere stop-gap; " $2 \cdot \xi^2 + \xi$ " is a pattern for deriving a designation of the function's value from a designation of its argument. Any complex symbol formed on this pattern will *contain* the sign of the function; such a symbol will, however, in no case *be* the sign of the function—it will always designate or indicate a number.

The function $2 \cdot \xi^2 + \xi$ is a numerical function; i.e. it takes numbers as arguments, and its value for a number as argument is again a number. But the values and arguments of a function need not be restricted to being numbers. A kind of non-numerical function that it will be specially useful to consider is a *linguistic* function (as we may call it); a function that takes names as arguments, and whose value for a name as argument is again a (complex) name. In his youthful work *Begriffsschrift* Frege explains the term " function " in general in a way that really fits only linguistic functions. ' Suppose that a simple or complex symbol occurs in one or more places in an expression . . . . If we imagine this symbol as replaceable by another (the same one each time) at one or more of its occurrences, then the part of the expression that shows itself invariant under such replacement is called the function; and the replaceable part, the argument of the function '.

By this explanation, there will be a certain (linguistic) function whose values for the numerals " 2 ", " 3 ", " 7 ", as arguments are

" 2.2^2+2 ", " 2.3^2+3 ", and " 2.7^2+7 " respectively. Now it seems right to say that it is this linguistic function that represents in language the numerical function $2.\xi^2+\xi$; we mention the numerical function by writing down some value or other of the linguistic function. (Observe that although $105=2.7^2+7$, the numeral "105", unlike " 2.7^2+7 ", is *not* a value of the linguistic function in question; so in writing down " 2.7^2+7 " we are mentioning the numerical function $2.\xi^2+\xi$, but in writing down " 105 " we are not.) So far as I know, Frege never explicitly adopts the view that linguistic functions are what symbolize numerical (or other) functions; but it seems likely that he would have adopted it if it had been put to him.

The same number may be the value of quite different functions, even for one and the same argument; thus, for the argument 1 the functions $2.\xi^2+\xi$ and $4-\xi$ both have the value 3. This is what makes non-trivial statements of equality possible. Frege insists that what is conveyed by mathematical equations is the strict identity of what is mentioned on either side of an equation; thus, $6:3=1+1$ because 6:3 is *the* number (not *a* number) which when multiplied by 3 yields the result of 6, and $1+1$ is that very number (since $(1+1).3=6$). What makes the equation informative is that though the same number is mentioned on both sides, it is presented as the value of two different functions—the quotient function and the sum function.

Frege carefully avoids the usual mathematical expression " the function $2.x^2+x$ "; for this would have gone against his view of how such mathematical symbolisms work. For him, " $2.x^2+x$ " or " x " itself, does not designate a function, but rather, indefinitely indicates a number. To be sure, " $2.x^2+x$ " *contains* mention of the function $2.\xi^2+\xi$; in our terminology it is the value of the corresponding linguistic function for the argument "x". Accordingly " $\vdash 2.x^2+x > -1$ " is an assertion concerning the function $2.\xi^2+\xi$—viz, that *its value* is always greater than -1. But it is not an assertion that *the function itself* is greater than -1; that would be nonsense. (Indeed, " $\vdash 2.x^2+x>-1$ " is really not so much an actual assertion about anything, as a schematic representation of the various assertions that can be got by using an actual numerical sign in place of the indefinite " x ".)

Mathematicians often identify a function with an ' indefinite ' or ' variable ' number or magnitude. Frege strongly objected to this.

To say that " x " or " 2 . x²+x " refers to an indefinite number in no way implies that there are definite numbers and indefinite numbers (no more than " King Charles of Sweden was shot by an unknown man " implies that there are two sorts of men, known men and unknown men); it is just a way of saying that these expressions refer to numbers indefinitely. Likewise, there are no variable numbers— a number does not wax and wane like the Moon. When we say e.g. that the number of children a man has increases with the years, we do not mean that besides the invariable numbers 1 to 6 there is a variable number, the number of the man's children, which ' assumes ' these ' values ' successively; we might as well suppose that there is a variable Sovereign of Great Britain, who really, not just by legal fiction, never dies, and who ' assumes ' to his person successively a middle-aged man and a young woman.

The temptation to identify a function with a variable magnitude arises especially over applied mathematics. A rod's length is a variable magnitude, and is also a function of the rod's temperature; have we not here, then, a function that is a variable magnitude? No; that is a ' fallacy of figure of speech '. " The length is a function of the temperature " does not imply " The length is a function "; it means rather that there is some function for which the length is *that* function of the temperature; if the rod is r mm. long at t° C., then we always have, for a certain function f( ), r=f(t).

Which function f( ) is must of course be discovered empirically; this probably strengthens the temptation—a point not mentioned by Frege. For people may well follow this confused line of thought: ' Which function it is, is not mathematically determinable; it must therefore be empirically observable; and what is empirically observable except one variable magnitude related to another? ' With this there would go the idea that there are empirical functions differing from those dealt with in pure mathematics. One might as well suppose that there are empirical numbers differing from the numbers dealt with in pure mathematics, because the answer to some questions of *how many* has to be got empirically.

A function, then, is not any sort of number or magnitude; and in fact, on Frege's view of functions, we find it impossible to supply the predicate " — is a function " with a subject so as to produce a well-formed and true statement. We cannot say " 2 . 3²+3 is a function " or " 2 . x²+x is a function " ; for 2 . 3²+3 is just the number 21, and, whatever number x may be, $2 . x^2+x$ is again a number, not a function. " $2 . x^2+x$ is a function of x " is all right, but does not imply " $2 . x^2+x$ is a function "; it rather means " There is a function f( ) such that, whatever x may be, $2 . x^2+x$ is *that* function of x—i.e. $2 . x^2+x=f(x)$ ". If we say " (the function) $2 . \xi^2+\xi$ is a function ", that is wrong too; for it could be right only if " $2 . \xi^2+\xi$ " were the name of a function, which, as explained above, is not so. If we tried leaving an empty place for the argument, and wrote " $2 .(\ )^2+(\ )$ is a function ", this would not be a well-formed sentence—and any way of filling up the brackets would again be wrong. ' We cannot avoid a certain inappropriateness of linguistic expression; . . . there is nothing for it but to realise this and always take it into account '.

Frege's view of functions here runs into paradox, and this has often been taken as a proof that it is wrong. Various remedies for Frege's troubles have been proposed. Carnap long ago suggested that instead of saying in Frege's style " There are numbers, e.g. 6, and functions, e.g. the factorial function $\xi!$ " we ought rather to say " There are numerical signs, e.g. " 6 ", and functional signs, e.g. " ! " " Similarly, more recent critics have explained Frege's ' mistake ' in some such way as this: ' Frege wanted to have every symbol stand for something; but since he realized that a sign like " ! " in " 6 ! " (" factorial 6 ") does not stand for something in the way that " 6 " stands for a number, he said it stood for a queer sort of entity—a function. If only he had realized that there are different sorts of symbol; that not every sort of symbol has to stand for something! As it was, he mistook a linguistic difference for a fissure in the bedrock of reality '.

Such treatment is quite superficial. Frege cannot have been misled in the way supposed; for consider how one and the same function is mentioned in the complex designations " $2 . 1^2+1$ " and " $2 .3^2+3$ ", or again in " $(2+3 . 0^2) . 0$ " and " $(2+3 . 1^2) . 1$ ", which are two of Frege's examples of functions; there is no recognisable functional sign, in either case, that can be picked out as " ! " can be picked out from " 6 ! "—there is nothing for Frege to have wrongly assimilated to a numeral. And these examples also show the futility of Carnap's recourse to language about language; for in these cases there is no sign that could be picked out to stand between quotes as subject of the predicate " — is a functional sign ". Nor would Frege allow such a statement as " " ! " is a functional sign " ; ' an

isolated functional symbol is a monstrosity ', and what really sym-
bolizes the function is not just the occurrence of " ! " but the circumstance that " ! " follows a numerical sign. (The sign of a function, I
have argued, *is itself a function*, and not an actual quotable expression;
if so, it is quite futile to try to make out " functional sign " to be a
more intelligible term than " function ".)

The ' unavoidable ' inappropriateness of language comes about
because of a grammatical similarity and logical dissimilarity between
the word " function " and e.g. " integer "; this is unavoidable only
in relation to our sort of language, and no corresponding inappropriateness exists in a well-constructed symbolism like Frege's. On the
other hand, the best symbolism cannot *informatively* state what a
function is; if you do not already grasp that, you will not see how the
symbolism works. These considerations of Frege's were what led
Wittgenstein in the *Tractatus* to treat the concept *function* as a
' formal ' concept, expressible not by a proper predicate but only by
a manner of symbolizing; it is only thus, in fact, that this concept is
expressed in Frege's symbolism. (And this is turn has an obvious
connexion with Wittgenstein's doctrine that what ' shows ', or comes
out, in language cannot be stated in language.)

Frege requires that every function shall have a determinate value
for any argument you care to mention; it is clear that otherwise we
should have a complex designation, correctly formed so as to designate
the value of the function for some argument, but not in fact designating anything; and such designations, as we saw, Frege holds to be
inadmissible in serious scientific discourse. Frege's requirement
seems reasonable enough if we take it just as excluding numerical
functions that would lack a value for some numerical arguments: it
is an instance of the ' wrong expressions ' and ' wrong thoughts ' in
ordinary mathematics that some such functions are left undefined
for some arguments—in Hardy's *Pure Mathematics* it is even stated
that there are pairs of functions differing in that one is defined for a
certain argument and the other is not! (The sort of instance Hardy
had in mind would be the functions 2ξ and $2\xi^2/\xi$, for the argument
0.) Frege naturally requires also that every function shall have *only*
one value for any given argument; otherwise we should get ambiguous
designations. Here too he is objecting to the practice of mathematicians (cf. my remarks at the beginning about " $\sqrt{4} = \pm 2$ ").

What may at first appear a less reasonable requirement is that if our discourse includes objects other than numbers, all the functions mentioned are to be defined for non-numerical as well as numerical arguments. Thus, if we are doing astronomy, and discoursing both about numbers and about heavenly bodies, then we must define e.g. the sum function so that we know what is the sum of the Moon and the number 2. Naturally this does not mean that there must be some algorithm by which we can work out the *right* answer to the question " What is $\mathbb{C}+2$? "; the answer is a matter of arbitrary stipulation; ' the only point of a rule to this effect is that there should *be* a rule '. What, then, is the point of having a rule at all? For Frege, every complex designation must have a reference, if it is well-formed; so we can deny a reference to designations like " $\mathbb{C}+2$ " only if we are going to have formation-rules that exclude them from our language. The framing of such rules in a watertight way is a much heavier business than stipulations which would supply a reference for this sort of designation—say, the stipulation that when the signs preceding and following the *plus* sign do not both stand for numbers, the whole expression has the same reference as the sign preceding the *plus* sign, so that " $\mathbb{C}+2$ " would designate the Moon, and " $2+\mathbb{C}$ ", the number 2.

We have so far considered only functions taking numbers and other objects as their arguments—*first-level* functions; there are also functions that take functions as their arguments—*second-level* functions. We must not suppose this term to mean what a mathematician commonly calls a function of a function, e.g. log sin ξ; for here we do not get the function log ξ taking the function sin ξ as argument; in e.g. " log sin $\pi/2$ " the argument-place of " log ξ " is filled up with a designation of *the value of* the function sin ξ for the argument $\pi/2$—in fact, a designation of the *number* 1. But we do get second-level functions in ordinary mathematics; one instance already mentioned is: the limit of $\phi(n)$ as n increases indefinitely. (This way of speaking is a vestige of muddled ideas about variable numbers; but a *definition* of the term "limit" in a good modern textbook would introduce no such confusion.) Just as we get a designation of a definite number out of " sin ξ " if we fill up the argument-place marked by " ξ " with an actual numeral, so we get a designation of a definite number out of " the limit of $\phi(n)$ as n increases indefinitely " if we substitute mention of an actual first-level function at the place where " $\phi( )$ " stands. Our term " linguistic function "

enables us to state this more precisely: what must be substituted for
" $\phi(n)$ " is the value, for " n " as argument, of a linguistic function
representing a numerical function. Thus, the xth power of $(x+1){:}x$
is a certain numerical function of x; the value for " n " as argument
of the corresponding linguistic function is " the nth power of $(n+1)$:
n "; and if we substitute this for " $\phi(n)$ " we get: " the limit of the
nth power of $(n+1)$: n as n increases indefinitely "—a designation
of the number *e*.

We can now understand Frege's use of " $M_\beta\phi(\beta)$ " as a general
symbol for a second-level function, where " $\phi(\beta)$ " occupies the
argument-place. If we want to symbolize a function of a definite
first-level function, we shall replace " $\phi(\beta)$ " with the value, for
" β " as argument, of the linguistic function symbolizing that first-
level function. " β " thus marks, at its second occurrence, an
argument-place in a symbol standing for, or indefinitely indicating, a
first-level function: and this first-level functional symbol itself
occupies the argument-place in a second-level functional symbol.
" The limit, as β indefinitely increases, of $\phi(\beta)$ " is an expression
constructed on the model of " $M_\beta\phi(\beta)$ "; the choice of " n " (as
above) or " β " is of course indifferent.

A specially important second-level function was the *value-range*
function: the value-range $\dot{a}F(a)$ was to be identical with the value-
range $\dot{a}G(a)$ if and only if the functions $F(\xi)$ and $G(\xi)$ always had
the same value for the same argument. In connexion with this
function, Frege introduced a first-level function of two arguments,
$\xi\frown\eta$: if y is a value-range, x$\frown$y is the value for x as argument of any
function whose value-range is y; since all functions whose value-
range is the same have the same value for any given argument, it
does not matter which function with the value-range y we take.
(On Frege's principles, the value of $\xi\frown\eta$ must be specified also for the
case when the second argument of the function is *not* a value-range.
This condition is easily satisfied: we might stipulate that whenever
y is not a value-range x$\frown$y=x. This was not in fact Frege's own
stipulation, but, as we have seen, all that matters is that there shall
be some stipulation.)

Frege is here using notions of great logical importance even in
contemporary work. (The functions in modern logic analogous to
Frege's $\dot{a}\phi(a)$ and $\xi\frown\eta$ are called *functional abstraction* and *functional*

M

application respectively.) But the doctrine of these functions, as stated by Frege, involves a contradiction.

This contradiction arises thus. We shall always have, on Frege's theory:

$$\vdash F(x)=\acute{x}\grave{a}F(a).$$

Let us then take an arbitrary function $G(\xi)$ and consider the function $G(\acute{\xi}\grave{\xi})$. This function will have its own value-range, $\grave{a}G(a\grave{a})$. Substituting in " $\vdash F(x)=\acute{x}\grave{a}F(a)$ " mention of the function $G(\acute{\xi}\grave{\xi})$ for mention of the function $F(\xi)$, we have:

$$\vdash G(\acute{x}\grave{x})=\acute{x}\grave{a}G(a\grave{a})$$

And substituting " $\grave{a}G(a\grave{a})$ " for " x " in the last assertion, we have:

$$\vdash G(\grave{a}G(a\grave{a})\grave{}\grave{a}G(a\grave{a}))=\grave{a}G(a\grave{a})\grave{}\grave{a}G(a\grave{a}).$$

The purport of this assertion is that, starting from any arbitrary first-level function $G(\xi)$, we can always specify in terms of it an argument—in fact $\grave{a}G(a\grave{a})\grave{}\grave{a}G(a\grave{a})$—for which the value of $G(\xi)$ is equal to that argument. But this conclusion is absurd; for we can specify any number of first-level functions whose value is *never* the same as the corresponding argument. Thus no second-level function will in fact exactly fulfil the role Frege assigned to his value-range function. How to mend Frege's system at this point is an important technical problem of logic; but it is of no philosophical importance how this is done.

In rejecting the old doctrine of subject and predicate, Frege maintained that it could fruitfully be replaced by a doctrine of function and argument. He began, as I mentioned before, by studying linguistic functions. When a proposition contains a name, it may be regarded as the value of a certain linguistic function for that name as argument; and in a language free from ambiguity, the same predication will be made in two propositions respectively relating to objects named "A" and " B " if one proposition is the value of a certain linguistic function for the argument "A" and the other is the value of the same linguistic function for the argument " B ".

Thus, " Brutus killed Caesar " and " Cassius killed Caesar " are values of a linguistic function for the arguments " Brutus " and " Cassius " respectively; " Brutus killed Brutus " and " Brutus killed Caesar " are values of a second linguistic function for the arguments " Brutus " and " Caesar " respectively; " Brutus killep

Brutus " and " Cassius killed Cassius " are values of a third function for the arguments " Brutus " and " Cassius " respectively. In all three cases the propositions that are values of the same function for different arguments serve to make the same predication about the objects named by the respective arguments; but only in the first case have we an expression occurring in the two propositions that would be recognised by grammar, or by ' traditional ' logic, as a common predicate; and in the last case it is patent that the common predication is not effected by the presence of a common expression, but rather by the two propositions' being formed on a common pattern.

This treatment of predication in terms of linguistic functions is clearly more general than the traditional treatment; in order to find a common predication in two propositions we need not alter their wording into an artificial standard form. Moreover, we are freed from the superstition about ' one subject and one predicate '. " Brutus killed Caesar " is at once the value for the argument " Brutus " of that function whose value for argument "A" is "A killed Caesar ", and the value for the argument " Caesar " of that function whose value for argument "A" is " Brutus killed A ". It is, just as it stands, *both* a predication about Brutus *and* a predication about Caesar; to suppose that taking it one way or the other makes it a different proposition is as absurd as it would be to think we could make two numbers out of 2+3 by regarding it now as the result of adding something to 2, now as the result of adding 3 to something.

As we saw, Frege's first notion of a function was one that fitted only linguistic functions; but he later came to think that this view was insufficient—that functions belong to the subject-matter, not just the notation, of mathematics; his mind passed from linguistic functions, whose values and arguments are numerical expressions, to numerical functions, whose values and arguments are numbers; so also it was natural that he should pass from the recognition of the linguistic functions that occur in predication to the view that there are functions in reality which these predicational functions represent. But here a difficulty arises which did not arise over numerical functions: if we take the complex expression that is the value of a linguistic function to be a designation of the value of a non-linguistic function, what is the value thus designated? If the values of a linguistic function are numerical expressions, then what is designated (or indefinitely indicated) will be a number; but the values of the linguistic functions involved in predication are propositions, which would ordinarily not be taken to designate anything at all; and Frege's looking for something that propositions stand for is often regarded as a misconceived assimilation of sentences to names, of asserting to naming.

Frege, however, sharply distinguished asserting from naming, as we have seen; the sentences that he would consider to be complex designations would in his symbolism not contain the assertion-sign. In ordinary language too we get unasserted propositions, occurring e.g. as clauses within assertions; Frege would certainly wish to analyse these as complex designations, but is not thereby confusing assertion with naming, for their role is certainly not that of making an assertion. It is indeed far from evident that (say) the clauses in a disjunction designate anything; but people will readily accuse Frege of confusion as to the role of such clauses when they have no positive account of that role to set against his.

Even an unasserted proposition, e.g. one thus occurring as a sub-clause, still has a truth-value—it is still appraisable as true or false. (It is quite absurd to say that such appraisals are possible only if a sentence is actually being used to make a statement.) A specially important class of context in which an unasserted proposition may occur is a truth-functional context; we may define a (linguistic) truth-function as a function whose values and arguments are propositions, the truth-value of the proposition that is its value being determined solely by the truth-value of its argument(s). The term is Russell's, not Frege's; but the use of it will make it much easier to expound Frege's doctrine. For instance, from any proposition " p " we may form a negation " not p ", of opposite truth-value; from any two propositions " p " and " q " we may form a disjunction " p or q ", which is false if both " p " and " q " are false and otherwise true; negation and alternation are thus truth-functions. (The propositions that are values of a truth-function, like those that are its arguments, should be taken as *un*asserted; for e.g. a negation or disjunction may occur as a sub-clause of an asserted proposition, without being itself asserted, and this in no way alters the sense of " not " or " or ".)

The importance of truth-functional contexts is that in mathematics we need not have one proposition occurring as a sub-clause of another except truth-functionally. Now to the question what is designated by such propositions, a simple answer was suggested to Frege by his study of Leibniz's formalized logic of identity. For Leibniz, an identity statement is true if and only if the expressions on either side of the identity sign are mutually substitutable in the propositions they occur in without changing the truth-value of such propositions. Conformably to this view, a proposition occurring truth-functionally as a clause will have *the same* reference as any other proposition of the same truth-value; for any such proposition will be substitutable for it *salva veritate*. Frege calls the common reference of all true propositions " the True " and that of all false propositions " the False ". Rather confusingly, he uses the term " truth-value " to mean, not only the truth or falsehood (as the case may be) of a proposition, but also the object designated by the proposition—the True or the False, as the case may be. The confusion is, however, only verbal; when Frege says that a proposition designates its truth-value, he means that if it is true it designates the True, not that if it is true it designates the fact that it itself is true.

This puts in a clearer light the role of the assertion-sign. In a language where the assertion-sign is used, a proposition that lacks the assertion-sign will in fact be a name of the True or of the False, but in writing it down we are so far not doing anything with it, no more than if we wrote down a designation of any other object; in Wittgenstein's phrase, we are only setting out the pieces on the board, not making a move in the game. What we do by writing the assertion-sign in front of the proposition is to *warrant it as* a name of the True; this is an entirely different performance from writing down any designation whatsoever.

Frege's talk about the True and the False may have the appearance of being concerned with a pair of peculiarly logical objects, discerned by some sort of intellectual intuition; and it is indeed possible that he himself was thus misled by his own way of speaking —as when he says: ' These two objects are recognised, if only implicitly, by everybody who judges something to be true—and so even by a sceptic '. But all that his theory really requires of the True and the False is that each shall be an identifiable object, distinct from the other; e.g., in a theory where all the other objects mentioned were numbers, we might take 0 to be the True and 1 to be the False.

Most asserted formulae will be correct or incorrect regardless of which object we take to be the True and the False. For example, an asserted formula obtained by filling up the blanks in " $\vdash(=)$ " with actual designations will be correct if and only if both designations stand for the same object. Accordingly, " $\vdash(2^4=4^2)$ " will be correct regardless of which object we take to be the True; " $(2^4=4^2)$ " is true, i.e. designates the True, if and only if " 2^4 " and " 4^2 " designate the same number, and the assertion-sign prefixed to the formula warrants it as designating the True. (On Frege's view as to the sense of assertions, since the *truth-condition* of the formula is independent of which object the True is, the *sense* also is so.) On the other hand, the correctness of " $\vdash(0=(2^4=4^2))$ " will depend on whether " 0 " and " $(2^4=4^2)$ " both designate the same thing, and therefore upon which object we stipulate as being the True, i.e. being designated by true unasserted propositions like " $(2^4=4^2)$ ".

We can now make Frege's view of concepts and predicates clear. A predicate is a linguistic function whose value, for a name of an object as argument, is always a complex designation of the True or the False, e.g. the expression " $D^2>2D$ " will designate the True or the False, whatever " D " is taken to designate, and is the value of a certain linguistic function for " D " as argument. The corresponding non-linguistic function $\xi^2>2\xi$ is a *concept* —the concept *having its square greater than its double*; this function has as its values: the True, for arguments that are objects falling under the concept, and the False, for all other arguments. (The objects falling under this concept are in any event the same, regardless of which objects the True and the False are taken to be.)

An apparent defect in Frege's ' function ' theory of predication is that it does not cover occurrences of predicates except in singular propositions, since Frege would not allow us to regard " Socrates is wise " and " every philosopher is wise " as values of the same function for the respective arguments " Socrates " and " every philosopher "; and again, how are we to account for the occurrence of the general term " philosopher " in " every philosopher is wise "? Frege would reply that logically the use of a general term, a ' concept-word ", like " philosopher ", is always predicative, and that we cannot see things clear till we have worked the sentence around to make this explicit. We shall come on to Frege's theory of generality (quantification) later on; but this sort of working-around is not difficult even in ordinary language—" Without exception, he who is a philosopher is wise ". Here we have the clauses " who is a philosopher " and " he is wise ", with indefinitely-indicating pronouns as their subjects; and these pronouns can be taken as arguments of the linguistic functions whose values for " Socrates " as argument are " Socrates is a philosopher ", " Socrates is wise ". In general, by such working-around we can get rid of ' subject '-occurrences of any general term, and have it occurring only to form clauses that are values of the corresponding linguistic function: the arguments of this function will always be either singular designations or indefinitely-indicating singular expressions like " he " or " who " (or again e.g. " whose father " in " Without exception, he whose father is a philosopher is a philosopher ".)

It is thus slightly misleading, on Frege's own principles, for him to speak of a general term as standing for a concept; what represents the concept is rather the structure of a clause with a singular subject and with that general term as predicate. (On the other hand, the way a singular name stands for an object is in no way dependent on that name's occurring in a special sort of clause). When a general term occurs non-predicatively in ordinary language, it ' stands for ' a concept only because it can be worked round into such predicative occurrence. All the same, Frege's use of the terms " concept-word, concept-expression " instead of " general term " are useful as marking his rejection of the old error that singular and general terms are alike names of objects, differing only in how many objects they name.

A more serious defect in Frege's way of expressing himself is his use of expression like " the concept *horse* ". Such expressions were of course introduced to stand for concepts—to answer such questions as " Which concept does the French concept-word " cheval " stand for? " They turned out, however, to be quite unsuitable for the purpose; for a phrase like " the concept *horse* " is not even significantly substitutable, let alone substitutable *salva veritate*, for the corresponding predicative use of " horse "; on the contrary, it is grammatically a singular term. Frege was misled by this fact into thinking that such phrases as " the concept *horse* ", and even such phrases as " what " (or: " the concept that ") " the concept-word " cheval " stands for ", do not stand for concepts but are singular names of objects; these objects somehow insist on going proxy for concepts in certain connexions, and in obtruding themselves as the subjects of our discourse instead of the concepts we want to talk about, so that we cannot say straight out what we mean but only hint at it!

It hardly needs saying that here Frege has simply got into a muddle. " The concept *horse* " would have to stand for a concept if it stood for anything; in fact it does not, and sentences in which it occurs are at best circumlocutory (" falls under the concept *horse* "= " is a horse ") and at worst philosophers' nonsense. Frege himself came to see the undesirability of such expressions. On the other hand, he would, at this later stage of his thought, have allowed such expressions as " what the French word " cheval " stands for "; but this must not be used as a singular name, but as a predicate substitutable *salva veritate* for " (a) horse " (" the animal in that cage is what the French word " cheval " stands for "), just as " what " Julius Caesar " stands for " is substitutable *salva veritate* for " Julius Caesar ". (This solution of Frege's difficulties was suggested by myself in 1951; I have now learned from Mr. Michael Dummett that Frege's posthumous papers contain the same solution.)

English grammar allows us to escape Frege's difficulties in yet another way: we may replace Frege's term " concept " by " kind of thing ". Instead of troubles as to whether the concept *horse* is a concept, we can say " horses are a kind of thing "; now Frege says that a general term in the plural without an article stands for a concept, i.e. for what I am calling a kind of thing, so this sentence is unexceptionable. Similarly for " the concept *dragon* is a concept (?) under which no object falls " we have " dragons are a kind of thing, but no object is that kind of thing", which again avoids the difficulty. And similarly instead of "The French word "cheval" stands for a concept.—Which concept?—The concept *horse*—only that is really an *object* which at this point thrusts itself forward instead of the concept we wanted to talk about! " we shall get: " The French word " cheval " stands for a kind of thing—Which kind of thing?— Horses "; and again, since " Horses " does stand for a kind of thing, there is no difficulty.

Where I have spoken of a kind of thing, logicians often speak of a class of things. This way of speaking Frege carefully avoided, because it has such very misleading suggestions (shared by the word " set "). A class is naturally thought of as composed of its members;

the natural way of referring to a class—its proper name, so to say—would be a list of its members; if instead we specify the class by using a general term "A" that is an exclusive common predicate of its members and calling the class " the class of all As ", that is a sort of *pis aller*. On this conception of a class, infinite classes are barely intelligible, and a null class flatly impossible; it is a wholly indefensible procedure (common as it is in logic books) to try to introduce a null class on this footing. Even when this conception is not initially used, the pull of the word " class " is very strong; thus, Russell uses " class " in his logical works in a sense not far removed from " concept " or my " kind of thing ", but when framing theories of matter he talks as though a class of sense-data were made up of sense-data.

To be sure, in cases where different predicates hold good of the same objects (including the case where none of the predicates applies to any object at all), logicians and mathematicians find it convenient to assume the existence of an object that is the *extension* of all these similarly-applied predicates. But no properties of an extension are useful, or are used, in logic and mathematics, except that two predicates which apply to just the same objects (or neither of them to any object) have the same extension, and that conversely (in all ' ordinary ' cases) two predicates with the same extension apply to just the same objects; it need not be assumed that in some way the extension of a predicate is made up of the things to which the predicate applies. Now Frege regarded predicates as representing a special sort of functions—viz concepts, i.e. functions whose value is always either the True or the False; and when predicates apply in the same way, the corresponding functions will for Frege always have the same value for the same argument. The functions $\xi^2=1$ and $(\xi+1)^2=2(\xi+1)$ are such a pair of functions; each has the True as its value for the arguments $+1$ and -1, and the False for all other arguments. It was natural, then, for Frege to identify the extension of a predicate with the *value-range* of the corresponding function.

At this point, of course, there becomes important the contradiction about value-ranges that I have already mentioned. Russell gave this contradiction an intuitive formulation in terms of " the class of all classes that are not members of themselves "; but a rigorous and simple formulation relating to value-ranges generally has already been given. The result of this is that only for ' ordinary ' predicates can we safely assume that two predicates with the same extension always apply to the same objects, and there will be ' odd ' cases in which this is not so. For our contradition requires for its resolution, if we accept Frege's other premises, some modification in his requirements concerning value-ranges; there must be ' odd ' cases in which two functions have the same value-range, but have not the same values for *every* argument. It could easily be shown that some of these ' odd ' cases will occur when the functions in question are concepts; which means that, though the predicates answering to the concepts have an identical (value-range as their) extension, the truth-values of the assignment of these predicates to objects will not always be the same. For if the concepts ξ *is* P and ξ *is* Q have different values for A as argument, then the assignments of the predicates " P ", " Q ", to A—i.e. "A is P ", "A is Q "—will have different truth-values. But further details of this difficulty belong to technical logic, and may here be omitted.

The importance of Frege's doctrine concerning extensions has been grossly exaggerated because it has been thought an essential part of his doctrine concerning numbers. But Frege explicitly states that the identification of numbers with certain extensions is only a secondary and doubtful point, and in stating his theory of numbers I shall ignore extensions altogether. (Cf. the *Grundlagen*, end of §107.)

Frege begins by rejecting certain plausible but erroneous views. Numbers cannot be physical properties of things, because (a) all sorts of things, not only bodies, can be counted; (b) neither 1 nor 0 can be explained as a physical property of things; (c) the same physical collection may be described in terms of different numbers—*four* boots may (or may not) be *two* pairs of boots. Neither can numbers be the mere creation of the mind, as Berkeley thinks; a hard-pressed officer cannot increase the number of his troops merely by taking thought. As for the view that arithmetic relates to operations on ' abstract units ', which are ' abstracted ' out of operations on ' concrete units ', it is grossly incoherent in all sorts of ways (popular as it now is with educationalists). From what operation with a concrete pair and trio, and by what abstractive process, could one come to understand " 2^3 "?

Frege's own constructive theses are that a number attaches to a concept, and that to assign a number is to ascribe a ' property ' to a concept. In spite of his clear explanations, he has been perversely taken to mean that an answer to the question ' how many ' is always a ' conceptual ' i.e. an analytic statement: which is clearly absurd, and was never his intention. All obscurity vanishes from the first thesis if we say: A number is a number of a *kind of things*. There may be none, or one, or many of a kind. When the same physical collection is said to be *two* pairs of boots, but *four* boots, it is because different kinds of things are being counted; but given the kind of things, the number is determinate, not a free creation of the mind.

As for the second thesis, it would indeed not do to call the number of a kind of things a ' property ' of that kind of things: but what Frege explains as his meaning may be put as follows: It is *incidental to* or *supervenient upon* any given kind of things, how many things of the kind there are. The mistake against which this thesis is directed is committed for example by Descartes, when he says in the Third Meditation that the ideas of God's several attributes could not have come into his mind from a plurality of beings who possess them piecemeal, because unity, simplicity, or inseparability of attributes is itself one of the attributes included in his idea of God. *That there is one and only one being who has* certain attributes is something *supervenient upon* those attributes, and cannot itself *be one of* those attributes.

We get here a new class of expressions, which serves to assign to an attribute (itself signified by a concept-expression) a *mode of occurrence*: to express the supposition that the attribute occurs universally, or in seven instances, or somewhere, or nowhere at all. Frege says that such expressions signify *second-level* (or *second-order*) *concepts*. The general characteristic of expressions for second-level concepts is that their sense is completable (to yield the sense of a clause) by adding an expression for a first-level concept—for a kind of things. Examples of such expressions are: " something or other is a— " (" there exists a— "); " all —s are land-dwellers " ; " there are at least three —s ". As regards the first example, Frege rightly stresses the importance of realising that existence (in that sense of the word which answers to " there is " or to German " es gibt ") is not a first-level concept, an attribute of things; he is saying that *there is no such kind of things as ' things that there are '*—a genus to which cows, but not dragons, would belong. Aristotle had said this long before; but logic was for a long time not sufficiently developed for his remark to be fully understandable.

For Frege, as I have said, a first-level concept is properly expressed in a clause that is a value of the corresponding linguistic function; accordingly, he wanted to replace the above sort of expressions for second-level concepts by ones in which the expression for a first-level concept that has to be inserted is not just a general term, but a corresponding clause with a singular (indefinitely-indicating) subject. He accomplished this aim by a notation that differs in no important respect from the modern quantifier-notation, in which for example, we get:

For " something or other is a— ": " for some x, . . . x . . ."

For "all —s are land-dwellers": "for any x, if . . . x . . . , then x is a land-dweller ".

In each case we get sense if we replace ". . . x . . ." by an actual clause containing the indefinitely-indicating singular term " x ". Such a clause may be formed by attaching a general term to " x " as its grammatical predicate, but we are not confined to such cases; it is clear that " $x^2+2x = 3$ " would make sense in the first example, and " x's mother is a land-dweller ", in the second. Thus the quantifier notation enables us to exploit to the full Frege's generalized notion of a predicate: we can use a value of any arbitrary predicational linguistic function so as to fill up the argument-place in an expression for a second-level concept. With this notation, a second-level concept is presented by an expression having the general form, " $M_\beta\phi(\beta)$ ", which Frege gives to second-level functions (the use of " x " rather than " β " is of course an irrelevant detail); this is as it should be, for a first or second level concept just is, in Frege's view, a first or second level function whose values are restricted to the True and the False.

Among second-level concepts we must now specially attend to those expressed by locutions of this type: " there are just as many —s as there are As ". As a preliminary to his account of numbers, Frege propounds an analysis of " there are just as many Bs as As ", which may be put as follows: For some interpretation of " R ",

(1) For any x that is an A, there is a y that is a B to which x is R.

(2) If x and y are As, and x is R to a given B, say z, and y also is R to z, then x is the same A as y.

(3) For any y that is a B, there is an x that is an A and is R to y.

(4) If y and z are Bs, and some A, say x, is R to y and is also R to z, then y is the same B as z.

Shortly: There is some *one-one* relation between As and Bs. This analysis, in spite of the word " one-one " (Russell's) which I have used for brevity, does not introduce any mention of the number 1 or of the concept *number*; so there is no risk of a vicious circle. To give a concrete example: A host knows that there are exactly as many guests as chairs in a room if (1) every guest is sitting on a chair; (2) two guests are not sitting together on the same chair; (3) every chair has a guest sitting on it; (4) no guest is sitting on two chairs at once! (And here again the use of the word " two " is inessential; (4) for example is short for " If y is a chair in the room, and so is z, and some guest, x, is sitting on y and also sitting on z, then y is the same chair as z.")

Frege's analysis has been criticized on the score that in empirical cases we should often establish that there are just as many As as Bs, not by finding or setting up a one-one correlation between As and Bs, but by counting the As and the Bs and getting the same number. But this is to forget that it is not essential for us to use numerals, i.e. words for numbers, so long as we only want to find out whether there are just as many As as Bs; we might use some arbitrary string of words learned by heart, say the rhyme ' Eany-Meany-Miny-Mo ', and observe whether we got as far along the string with the As as with the Bs. What we are doing is to set up a one-one correlation between a set of words and the As, and again between the same set of words and the Bs; but then automatically we also set up an (indirect) one-one correlation between As and Bs. The objection thus disappears.

Having analysed " there are just as many As as Bs " in a way that involved no mention of numbers or of the concept *number*, Frege can now offer this analysis as a criterion for numerical identity—for its being the case that the number of As is the same number as the number of Bs. Given this sharp criterion for identifying numbers Frege thought that only prejudices stood in the way of our regarding numbers as objects. I am strongly inclined to think he is right.

One prejudice that perhaps deserves special mention is the idea that an object must be picturable. But why should we not say that * * * is a picture of the number 3 just as a police photograph is a picture of Bill Sikes? In either case it is not enough to have the picture, one must *learn to use it*; but the recognition of the number 3 from the picture * * * is far easier and more certain than the identification of Bill Sikes from the police photograph, and indeed the concept *the same number* less problematic than the concept *the same man*.

A certain uneasiness remains; I can only conclude with what Wittgenstein reported to me as Frege's words to him at the end of their last meeting. Asked whether he never saw *any* difficulty in the view that numbers are objects, Frege replied: " Sometimes I *seem* to see a difficulty; but then again I *don't* see it."

The technical terminology of Frege has here been rendered as in *Philosophical Writings of Gottlob Frege*, Blackwell, 1952.

I have deliberately omitted from this account of Frege any discussion of a peculiar doctrine of sense and reference, which relates to a puzzle about *oratio obliqua* clauses: viz that within them two designations of the same object are no longer substitutable for each other *salva veritate*. To take one of Frege's examples: If " a " and " b " are short for two different ways of designating the same object, then:

" It is worth while to be informed that a=b " may be true, whereas:

" It is worth while to be informed that a=a " will pretty certainly be false.

Frege concluded that in these *oratio obliqua* contexts " a " and " b " do not have their ordinary reference, but each of them stands for a peculiar entity—an ' oblique reference ' which Frege identified with the ' ordinary sense ' of " a " or " b ", as the case may be; thus he avoids the apparent violation of Leibniz's law that designations of the same thing are mutually replaceable *salva veritate*. Again, the *oratio obliqua* clauses " (that) a=b " and "(that) a=a" are designations, not of the True, but of two different ' thoughts ' (a word that must be taken to mean *that which is* thought, not a psychical event).

This theory is both sketchy and obscure; in much of Frege's work it hardly appears—which is not surprising, for in much formal logic there occurs no *oratio obliqua* such as the theory was designed to apply to. In fact, Frege never worked out this theory far enough to have to consider how it should be symbolically expressed. The fact that in America some people treat this theory as an important first step towards a ' rigorous ' semantics, and pretty well ignore Frege's account of functions, is just the latest chapter in a sad story of neglect and misunderstanding.